THE
ROBES
OF
FAILURE

BY

ANDREW DARRAGH

The Contractor's Prayer

*Dear Lord, please let there be another big contract and
I will promise not to piss it up against the wall like
I did with the last one. Amen.*

For Billy and Rab, Gone but not forgotten.

PREFACE

A philosophy professor stood before his students and placed a large empty glass jar on the table. He then produced a bag of rocks and poured them in. He put the lid on and asked them if it was full. They agreed and so the professor removed the lid and produced a bag of pebbles. He poured them in and they rolled into the open areas between the rocks. He put the lid back on and asked the same question. The students agreed that the jar was indeed full. The professor took the lid off again a produced a bag of sand. He poured it into the jar and it filled the areas left by the pebbles. He put the lid on and again he asked if the jar was full. The students responded with a unanimous 'yes'. Finally, the professor produced two bottles of beer. When he removed the lid and poured them into the jar the students burst into laughter. Once they had returned to silence he said, "This jar represents your life. The rocks are your important things like your faith, your health, your family and friends. The things that if everything else was lost, your life would still be full. The pebbles are things that matter next like your house, your car and your job. The sand is all the rest of the mundane stuff you have to deal with. Now if you put the sand first then there will be no room for the important things. Get the priorities right. Keep your faith, look after your health take time to love your family and help your friends. There will always be time to fix the house, drive the car and go to work. As for the rest then it's just sand. Are there any questions?"

"What about the bottles?" shouted one of the students.

"Ahh yes," began the professor. "Remember, no matter how full your life is, there is always room for a few beers."

The book you are about to read is about a year I spent working on an off-shore platform in the UK before moving on to an onshore production facility in Kazakhstan. The people in this book are real and so are the stories. So like the professor said, grab a few beers and switch off for a while.

TRIP ONE

SUNDAY JANUARY 1ST

I t is a cold dark night in January and all the clocks were striking twelve. I know that Big Brother maybe watching, but what the hell. The year is but a few seconds old and I am looking at it from the cellar deck of an oil rig in Morecambe Bay. I am on a twelve thousand tonne platform that is currently dwarfed by two jack-ups called 'The Bay Driller' and 'The Morecambe Flame'. The real reason they are both here is due to the fact that this platform was nowhere near ready when it came out here and we have been playing catch-up ever since. Just over twenty miles away the lights of Blackpool flicker in a new year. To my right is darkest Wales, to my left is deepest Cumbria and behind me is a distant Ireland. The white horses below me tumble beneath a glowing flare as the pipelines beneath it all pump gas to the shore. I'm offshore, four days into a three-week trip, and as the nation celebrates, I stand alone to contemplate what lies ahead. I don't get too far before our electrical foreman charges past me cursing about a work permit he has forgotten to sign off.

"Happy New Year, Trevor!" I shout.

"Fuck off, bigun," he replies. Not the best first foot I've had but he has a point. He doesn't want to be here right now and neither do I, but I can't complain. It's the industry I have always wanted to be part of and I am well aware of the sacrifices you have to make. At the same time I also knew that if I could stick it out and do my bit then one hell of life lay before me. It's all in the mind, I say to myself. Rise above it and never sink below it. As the wind begins to bite I turn and head back towards the accommodation module.

"Good night, bigun," a distant voice shouts.

"Fuck off, Trevor," I reply. Doublethink away, I'm off to bed.

MONDAY JANUARY 2ND

A normal rota runs two weeks offshore and the two weeks onshore. It's a set pattern unless you are changing rotas for special occasions, etc. I am currently on a three-week trip as I had Christmas off. When you are on leave your job is covered by your 'back to back' or 'btb'. The shifts usually run from 6.00am through to 9.00pm. You get an hour for lunch and the same for your evening meal. In between that it's all about reaching milestones and so the work tends to be head down, arse up. I'm working for the completions team that is responsible for all system handovers from construction to commissioning and then onto operations. In addition to all that, we have certifying authorities like Lloyds Register to keep happy so their surveyors are always with us.

Today was all about punchlist clearance. A punchlist is a list of outstanding work you attach to something when you try and hand it over to them. In our game the items fall into two categories, 'Cat A' means it's not safe so it has to be fixed. 'Cat B' means it's minor so you can operate it and it can be fixed later. It's not something you use in the real world. You don't exactly go into a car show-room to pick up your new car and have a salesman there with a punchlist. 'Sorry sir, your BMW will be a few days late as the steering wheel is missing (Cat A)." Or, "There you go sir, all yours."

"Hang on, what about the scratch across the door?" you say.

"Oh that, well that's just a Cat B' item, isn't it?" You would go somewhere else, wouldn't you? If that mentality was used offshore then nothing would get done.

TUESDAY JANUARY 3RD

Crew change is back to normal and Bobby our painting inspector calls in with a newspaper. He lets me know what a great time he had over the holidays and then he told me a funny little story about a little work trip he had to do.

He had to spend two days in Norway to watch a new shot blast and painting technique that one of the project contractors wanted to use offshore. Bobby had no intention of wasting two full days on it so he set it up so that the full test would be done on day one and then he could get bladdered good and early. He would have a long lay on day two followed by some sightseeing, a brief trip to site and then a flight home.

Day one and Bobby gets off the flight and goes straight to site. The test is all done by 4.00pm and so Bobby asks one of the girls to book him a taxi. The plan is to drop the bags off at the hotel and then go out on the lash. He is told that the car will be at the gate in fifteen minutes. Bobby gets some fags from the newsagent at the front gate and plonks himself down on a nearby bench. A moment later a local plonks himself on the other end. A car turns up with a big number written all over it accompanied by a row of mixed up letters. Bobby grabs the bags, opens the boot, throws them in and then jumps in the back seat. To his dismay the local from the bench is sitting in the front passenger seat. Bobby then tears into him and the driver, both of whom who don't speak much English. The argument gets so heated that Bobby is going to lamp them both. The guy behind the wheel panics and runs into the newsagent. As Bobby gets the other guy by the throat the door flies open. Standing hand on hips is the newsagent with said driver cowering behind him. "You speak English?" he asks just so that Bobby can fill the air with every expletive he knows. Once he lets go of the guy in the front seat and calms down the newsagent announces, "This gentleman here is a driving instructor, that a gentleman there is waiting to have his lesson, and you are stopping them."

WEDNESDAY JANUARY 4TH

The food offshore; Now let's be honest the food you get offshore is generally very good. To listen to some miserable gits though, you wouldn't think so. These are the people who have menus on the meal table at home. The wife standing over them asking are they ready to order. These are the people you see leaving the galley offshore after eating their own body weight in one sitting. The ones that pass you with a serviette full of cakes and a few pieces of fruit. The same ones that always reply, "Shite," when you ask, "What's on today?" Maybe it's because the meals are things people look forward to during the day and sometimes they don't meet their own private standards. For me I can't see what the issue is. At breakfast you can either have a cooked meal or cereals. At lunch and dinner there is always a meat, fish or pasta choice with all the usual veg and salad available. When I think about it, maybe there is some shite offshore and it's not the food. Today was a good day for cry-babies.

THURSDAY JANUARY 5TH

Dog and pony shows first began in the nineteenth century. There were small performing troupes run on a meagre budget which generally showcased unimpressive acts. They were predecessors of what we now know as a circus. The meaning has lost its way over the years as now it's used to describe lame presentations or poor managerial pitches.

The big weekly meeting on this project is known as 'The Dog and Pony Show'. Every Thursday the onshore-based managers come out to the platform to interrogate and drill us all on what we have not achieved, what we should achieve and how we should go about achieving it. They really are pathetic events. It means you have to spend most of each Wednesday making sure you have all the right facts and figures for them. The only thing these people deserve is fog.

FRIDAY JANUARY 6TH

I was right in the middle of a meeting on structural area completion when a familiar head popped around the door. "Oooooooiiiiiiiiiiiinnnnnnnnnkkkkk." John, one of our quality assurance inspectors is back. To everyone in the game he has always been known as 'Oink' because he uses that word all the time in sentences. I once asked him where it all began and he said it was all down to a time-served tradesman he used to be an apprentice to. One day this guy hit his thumb with a hammer and when he squealed, John said it sounded like the word "Oink." From that moment on he wound him up with it and then it just stuck. When anyone sees him they just shout "Oink" and he replies in the same manner. Like I said, he uses it all the time regardless of what forum he is in and who he is taking to. He's a bundle of fun and he helps you get through a trip with a few laughs. When you first meet him though it can be a little off-putting, but after that it's good to see the reaction of other first timers. I have been in a few meetings offshore with onshore management present when one of them will try and interrogate him on a matter of quality. "John, how many punchlist items are outstanding?"

"On category A we have sixty oink and on category B we have two hundred." Everyone that knows him doesn't batter an eyelid. Some people even nod. You then look at the guy who asked the question and you can see his brain going into overdrive. You know that he's asking himself about hearing the word and you wait to see if he is going to question it. If they ignore it and add a supplementary question he will do it again. Pretty soon they give up.

SATURDAY JANUARY 7TH

The offshore store or shop is called 'The Bond'. It's where you can buy things like toiletries and the offshore currency of Coca Cola and Mars bars. Alcohol is not allowed on offshore installations so if you celebrate something or want to say thank-you then you do it with soft drinks and chocolate. It's also where you buy duty free cigarettes or cigars. They are much cheaper offshore so you see smokers throwing them around like confetti. As we are only a few miles offshore, by law we can't bring any back in but those kind people in Customs and Excise have granted the project a concession. They have allowed you to bring either forty cigarettes or five cigars in. So naturally the fag gang buy sixty on the last day then open one packet and smoke one from it. That's now forty sealed and nineteen open so that doesn't count, does it? Same can be said for the la-di-dah gang. I don't smoke so I take in five King Edwards, for one of my uncles. On your last day offshore you always get someone who goes around everyone on your flight asking if they are taking anything in. If not, then it's do me a favour time.

SUNDAY JANUARY 8TH

We were all given safety t-shirts for one million man hours of safety. Basically if you get by without someone having an 'LTI' or 'Lost Time Incident' then you are doing really well. The safety offshore has increased immensely over the years and although it's only a t-shirt it's a measure of how far we have come. Now some guys just call them shite but when asked they never give them away. Others appreciate it and will wear it at work. Some like me appreciate it but give it away for someone else to use. Mine went to Joe, one of the Philippino men working on the barge. He was so grateful he invited me to his gambling night. I tried to decline but he was having none of it. I had to be in the quiet lounge at exactly ten minutes after eight and I had to bring £10 in £1 coins. I turned up just before my allotted time and the room was packed. It was like something out of a movie. He had people screaming odds and bets and money was changing hands everywhere. Anyway, I hear, "Mr Andy!" and then I was clapped to a table in the middle of the room. Joe was sitting opposite me with a small circular cup in his hand. Before me was a sweet jar full of small hard green beans. I placed my coins on the table. Joe took one from me and mimed what I had to do. I opened the jar and grabbed a large hand full of beans and placed them on the table. I then had to pick a number from zero, one, two or three. Joe had shown me the cup he had and it would hold four beans. I then realised what the game was. He was going to remove four beans at a time with the cup. In the end, if seven were left he would remove four and the winning number would be three. If six, he would remove four at the winner is two. If five, he would remove four and the winner is one. If exactly four are left he would remove them all and zero wins. Everyone in the room bets on the game but whatever number I pick would get special odds for anyone else that bets on it.

Ten minutes later, I stood up without any coins left. What I witnessed was an artist at work. Joe's hand-to-eye co-ordination was superb. The speed at which he removed the beans was just a blur to me. And while all this was going on the room was in uproar.

MONDAY JANUARY 9TH

"Four o'clock," was the first thing I said to him. It was Alan, a young tiffy, and he had been using my phone to call home. The lads on the tools don't have the same access to phones as we office wallers so when you see someone at your desk, you give them a moment. My head was too deep into an as-built drawing to notice Alan at first. When I did eventually stumble upon him he looked up from the phone with tears in his eyes. I said nothing and retreated to a tea point in the corridor. A few moments later he came along and thanked me. "Four o'clock," I said. He just looked puzzled so I asked, "Son or daughter?" He told me that it was his young son and he wanted to know when he was coming home. I already knew the last bit. I told him the story about when I used to call home from a platform in the North Sea. My daughter Elizabeth was very young at the time so I used to try and call late at night as she had a habit of picking up the extension. There was many a night that I would end a call with the same tears in my eyes. "Why are you not here?" she once asked.

"So I can get lots of pennies for you," I replied thinking I was smart.

"Then why not just get a few pennies and come home sooner?" How do you answer that? The worst was always when you were asked, "What time are you coming home?" One night after a soul-destroying call I was sitting with tears in my eyes when an old boy opposite me just said, "Four o'clock. The next time she asks just say that." Sure enough a few nights later, while speaking to my wife Jayne on the phone, a little voice cut in. We had the usual chat and then Elizabeth asked, "When are you coming home?"

"Four o'clock," I replied.

"Ok," she said and then put the phone down on me. Alan laughed and told me he was going to try it. I didn't tell him the story for that. It was just letting him know that he wasn't the only silly bugger offshore.

TUESDAY JANUARY 10TH

A pipeline inspection gauge or 'pig' is used for the inspection and maintenance of a pipeline. You insert the pig into a pig launcher, and using the pressure driven flow of the product in it, you send it away until it reaches the receiving trap at the other end. A cleaning pig has disks that rub against the inside of the pipe to remove sediment or scale and magnets to attract and remove any loose objects. We need to send one soon but before that the maintenance team has a little bit of work left to do on our launcher. So the critical path has turned to its runway beam. A team from the management have just arrived on-board and our gaffer is one of them. We know what his first question will be so that's where Polish Pete, the commissioning planner, comes in. Pete is from London but his wife is from Poland and he is fluent in her language. With that in mind we get Pete to fill out the acceptance certificate from the beam in Polish. I insert a blank tape in the deck beside me, and my colleague Billy puts the cert in his reject tray. The moment has arrived. Phil our gaffer walks in, we all greet him, he sits next to Billy and I set the tape to record. This is how the certificate part went.

"Is that beam done?"

"No it isn't."

"Why not?"

"Because of that daft Polish mechy in commissioning, that's why." Billy hands Phil the certificate and he begins to study it.

"What's wrong? It has all the right deflections and it's in tolerance?"

"Read it properly," says Billy. Phil then starts to look more closely at the words. We then got one of the best responses ever.

"What the fuck is this? Just what the fucking hell is this? I've seen some stupid things in my time but this just takes the cake. Who does he work for, the fucking John fucking Cleese agency? Fancy bringing a fucking foreign bastard out here who can't speak a cunting word of bastard English. We're not accepting that. The project twatting language is fucking bastard English for God's sake." I still have the tape.

WEDNESDAY JANUARY 11TH

We have a new addition to the completions team. Glen is our new technical clerk. Whether you like it or not within the first five minutes of meeting him you know that he likes karate and he has an original Rolex Oyster watch. He even has the box and guarantee to prove that it's a real one. It's not a fake and it's not a real fake as the black market traders called it, it's a real one. No sooner was that settled than Oink walked into the office. Within minutes, Glen is a sparrow-legged ninja with a trick watch. The ninja is now sitting before a cup of coffee, wondering what the hell was happening. If he was in any doubt, Oink put him right by lifting up his coffee cup and farting in it. That's when they both ran out of the door.

THURSDAY JANUARY 12TH

The laundry system offshore never ceases to amaze me. All the wives and mothers we leave behind onshore who separate whites from colours and delicates from everything else would go mental here.

All rooms come with meshed laundry bags that have the bunk numbers scribbled on them. It's your job to make sure you have the right one when filling it with gear. You drop it off in the laundry room and within twenty-four hours some of it makes its way back onto your bunk. It sounds ok so far, doesn't it? Right, let's go through what happens during that middle bit. Your entire bag either gets tossed into a machine along with many others or the items are removed and then get speared together with gigantic safety pins. Just in case anything breaks lose the lads in there have carefully written your bunk number on all the labels in your clothes. After that the machine then gets lined with a tonne of washing powder it is set to "Boil the life out of this lot" and it's left to run for hours. Initial torture over, your gear is then sent for a slow kill in the drying machines.

Back at the bunk you then get to peel your clothes apart. Your tops look and feel like empty crisp packets. Your trousers have the feel and smell of empty pizza boxes and your underwear has the welcoming look and feel of snot-filled tissue paper. You always know someone in newly-laundered gear as he usually looks like a window licker that has lost his bus and shuffles around as if he has just shit himself.

Now if you care, if you really care, you can pay the lads and they will iron it super stiff for you. That way you don't move like you have filled your pants, you just shuffle about like Douglas Bader instead.

FRIDAY JANUARY 13TH

I have seen many a violent mood swing over the years in this industry but none ever matches that of Mother Nature. Today was such a day. We spent the morning in the warmth of her bosom wrapped against a slight chill that whirled around us. As midday approached she turned on us and gave us the back of her hand. It was KBob one of our Quality Assurance engineers that spotted it first. His name is Bob but he has a slight speech impediment and the doctors told him to use the letter 'K' when struggling on a word. So for example he would say "Good morning, Kgents." Once he told everyone what the doctors had advised he then got called KBob instead of Bob. He's a kind-hearted soul and took no offence to it and if he did, no-one would give a toss anyway so he just got on with it. While we were on the main deck he looked out to the west and saw a pinstripe wall of bother rolling towards us. "It's time to get the Kstorm jackets out." It was on us before we knew it. The wind rose and then it quickly launched a deluge of rain. Pretty soon we were walking at forty-five degrees across the deck. The waves just got higher and higher. All non-essential work permits got pulled and several safety announcements came out over the tannoy system. It wasn't my first time and I was sure it wouldn't be my last. I have worked in the Brent fields of the North Sea and the weather there takes some beating, but when all is said and done, wherever you are it really is a site to behold. You can even feel the platform rock as Mother Nature slams into it. Wall upon wall of white water feverishly punches away at the jacket structure below you. As the spray from each impact fountains its way up through the grating on the decks you just hope that those clever structural people that designed it got their calculations right.

SATURDAY JANUARY 14TH

It's not the done thing to measure days offshore. I once remember one new guy made the mistake of placing a calendar on his wall and on his first shift put a big red cross on it. "Well fourteen to go," he announced. The next morning another big red cross was followed by, "Well that's thirteen to go." Two minutes later one of the old boys went to his desk, ripped the calendar of his wall, tore it to shreds and threw it all over him. That was the end of that.

The only allowable concession is when you know someone is getting to the end of their trip so you can ask, "When are you away then?" The standard answer is usual in measurements of 'gerups'. It's common to hear, "Two gerups and a gerup and go," Or, "Just a gerup and go." Such answers are always delivered with a smile. So when I was asked this morning I was able to beam and say, "One gerup and a gerup and go." It was all because of the drillers.

SUNDAY JANUARY 15TH

So the drillers have got one of their drill bits stuck down a well and they need a specialist team to come out and help retrieve it. That means ten people have to leave the platform. I am one of the chosen, along with Oink. Great, we think, we can go home early. We then find ourselves before the Construction Manager and are informed that the company want to put a selection of team members through a fire-fighting course. It means five days in Montrose, and before we ask we have already been booked on it. Bags are packed, survival suits are on, the safety video has been watched, the fifteen-minute flight is over, the Customs search has been completed and before we know it we are on a train up north.

MONDAY JANUARY 16TH

It's day one of the fire-fighting course in Montrose and the big roughy toughy firemen that stand before our class are about to tell us what we are about to go through. In between watching videos on the damage fires can do, we are going to don the required uniforms and put out a few small fires with a variety of extinguishers. Firstly, it's identification time and we all have a blank folded piece of card in front of us, and a pen. We are told to write our first names only so that we can be targeted with questions. Oink and I are on the back row and to our left are four BP engineers from Japan that don't speak a word of English. Not a problem, John assures the fireman, as apparently he has spent some time there and knows a bit of the lingo. As the rest of us set about writing our names, Oink and the Japs form a huddle. Job done, we settle down to a video on house fires and that's immediately followed by a question and answer session. After lunch it's more videos on various industrial type fires and then more talk followed by romper suit time. We are taken outside to the fire pad where we get to have a go with water, dry power, and foam and CO_2 extinguishers. We then end the day with a lessons learnt session. As we leave the class I wonder as to why the Japs never got asked a question. The answer soon became apparent when I looked at their cards. What fireman in his right mind would possibly want to converse with names like 'Shithead', 'Arseclamp', 'Fuckwit' and 'Boffball'.

TUESDAY JANUARY 17TH

It's day two and it starts with Oink betting all the class that before we leave on Friday he will have each of the Japs speaking one full meaningful sentence in English. The book is opened and odds are set. We then settle down learn about a century of fire. We are shown video clips, pictures and reports. It all makes for a solemn morning. Apparently, for it to be classed as an official disaster, twenty-five people have to die. 1903 USA Chicago, Iroquois Theatre 602 dead. 1913 Glamorgan Wales, Mine 439 dead. 1961 Brazil Niteroi, Circus 323 dead. 1980 Jamaica Kingston, nursing home 157 dead. Just a few examples of how quickly a fire can get out of control. If they wanted my full attention then they just got it. Lunch is followed by a little stroll in full uniform with a BA set on our backs. The stroll turns into a jog and is quickly followed by climbing in and out of buildings and carrying bodies. Whistles are going off everywhere as we all start to run out of oxygen through the sheer exertion of it all. We are eventually rounded up and asked to remove our face masks once we are out of air. One by one we go until there is a last man standing. Another few minutes pass before a fireman checks his gauge. Last man has still got half a bottle of air left. The puzzled fireman pulls his mask and asks him what he does for a living. "I am a diver," he calmly replies.

WEDNESDAY JANUARY 18TH

It's day three and Oink is in a huddle with the Japs again. No videos this morning just a quick run through on how we are going to walk into a fire with just an open fanned hose for protection. Before we know it we are out on the pad looking at a force fed fire wall. There are two hoses run out in parallel on the floor. We are told to get into two lines. Joe Soap here is at the front of one with Oink cowering behind me. A fireman points to a small valve at the foot of the wall. All we have to do is get to it and close it. We test the hoses and then move forward, making sure that we keep the line. As we close to the flames we open the hoses to their full extent and two overlapping fans of water appear. We keep moving forward. The flames start to whip around me and I just pray that the water keeps coming. The closer I get the more violent the flame. Eventually it has nowhere to go and so it attempts to get down the centre of the hose I am holding. The ferocity and pressure is unnerving and every now and then I hear a fireman whisper over my shoulder, "Hold your nerve." I hold it long enough for Oink to reach down and close the valve. As the flames die we retreat in a controlled manner. I switch the hose off and get a pack on the back from someone. "Nice one, Oink," I say.

"They don't fucking pay them enough, do they?" he replied. I couldn't give him an argument.

THURSDAY JANUARY 19TH

It's day four and once Oink has finished with his huddle we can get going. We start by getting our gear on, complete with BA, and go and sit in a room while someone sets fire to it. As we sit on the floor a fireman calmly explains its impact on mind and body. We then get shown the fireman's walk, back of one hand along the wall with the other sweeping up and down in front of you. As you perfect this you then shuffle forward. The reasons are then explained. Back of the hand because if its gets burnt you still have the grip side of your hand. The sweeping hand and shuffled feet are for any objects you may encounter in a smoke-filled room. A bit like the one we were now sitting in. We then form a chain, find a wall and then shuffle around it until someone finally reaches a door. We then get to crawl through the same room so that we can see the air pocket on the floor. Better still they then take your BA set off you and make you do it all again. After that we go for a climb around a nearby module. Lunch is followed by more climbing, more smoke-filled rooms and more fire. As the session ends we meet a Fire Chief who tells us that tomorrow they are going to set fire to the whole module. Everything we have learnt so far will be put to the test.

Friday January 20th

It's the last day. Oink has a final huddle and the fireman running the final exercise is looking for a valve man. He wants some nutter to lead a team on the top of the module and then descend two flights of fire, smoke-filled rooms and bodies to find a little valve. It's not just any little valve though. The gas going through it is feeding a fire on the ground floor and if it doesn't get closed the team down there can't clear the required rooms. I put my hand up. When asked who is going to be my support man I nominate Oink. The colour drains from his face. We are told that the current record for completing the entire exercise is fifty-seven minutes. I couldn't give a toss about that. I was tired and I just wanted to get on with it and go home.

The whole module was ablaze. I was given the nod so I grabbed a hose. Behind me were Oink and another two nutters. We had to get the valve and they had to take out the two bodies we had to find on the way to it. Hose tested ok, we began to move at pace. I cooled the access stairs and we raced up them. Once on the roof we reach the access hatch for the levels below. We hand in our ID clips to the fireman marker and I pull the hatch open. Smoke billows out from it. I let it ease and then spray the ladder with water. The steam rises; I pass the hose to Oink and climb down. Before I manage to tap the ladder to let him know I'm clear he soaks me in water. They all follow me down and we all eventually regroup at the bottom, I get the hose back and we move off around the walls. I spray away, clear obstacles and find the first body. Nutters three and four take it back up top. Down another level I find the next one. Nutters three and four take it and at the same time yank the hose away from me. Out of nowhere a fireman appears. "Keep moving," he tells me. "You are almost there." I push on through the smoke. The heat is intense. My gloves are smouldering against the wall, my feet feel like they are burning and the sweat is pouring out of me. At last I find it and call out to Oink. "Switch it off and let's get the fuck out of here!" he screams. Job done, we make our way back up top. Not having a hose we had to race up the steaming ladders. As we get a breather up top I think back to what Oink had said on Wednesday. He was right, they don't pay them enough.

Showered and changed we go back to the class to receive our certificates from the Fire Chief. "Oink," John says as he gets his.

"Thank you for letting me know," was the best thing I could come up with.

"What a load of bollocks," says Shithead.

"Just a bunch of tossers," says Arseclamp.

"Giz the fucker then," says Fuckwit.

"Can we please fuck off now?" says Boffball. As a puzzled chief looks on we all line up again in front of Oink and start handing him the money. Well that's the first trip of the year over.

Trip Two

Wednesday February 8th

Frank from the operations team rang and asked if I would bring out some mail for him. He then gave me the address of his tree-hugging eco-friendly brother call Ben. It was only twenty miles away so I called Ben and introduced myself. One hour later I was at his front door. He welcomed me into his kitchen and poured me a cup of herbal tea. As I took my first mouthful of something that smelt like cow shit and tasted of cough medicine, I noticed the piles of paper on the kitchen table.

There were ten self-addressed company envelopes with their contents neatly placed beside them. It was all kinds of junk mail, a mixture of special offers and deals, etc. As we chatted Ben proceeded to put the contents back into the envelopes and seal them. When I asked what he was doing he just said that if they can all send junk mail to him then he can send it to them. I just laughed. A double glazing company was about to be offered a loan from one of those high interest shark companies and a car dealer was going to get a perfume catalogue. It was mind boggling really; anyway after he gave me Frank's mail he also passed me the junk and asked me to post them. I smiled and agreed and then he remembered something else and brought a few more envelopes. They were bills he had forgotten to pay. When I reminded him that the envelopes didn't have any stamps on them he said he never used them when making a payment.

He knew the envelope would just be accepted anyway. Somehow we then got into a discussion about first and second class stamps. He reckoned we were all mad for using first class. His argument was that if more of us used second class stamps our mail would end up getting their just about the same time as the smaller amount of first class stuff. I was going to ask the obvious question but my head was starting to hurt and my mouth felt like a cat had been sleeping in it. I said my farewell and then got on with what time I had left.

After a goodbye from the kids and one last lingering hug from the wife it was into the hire car and off to Blackpool. I was leaving a little earlier as heavy snow-fall had been forecast and the police were going to close the notorious A66 Trans Pennine route between Scotch Corner and Cumbria. I got there just as the patrol cars began to block the road. "Take it easy son," they warned and let me by. As I looked in the rear view mirror, just two more cars were let through. So that was it, three of us crawling along with the snow getting deeper and the wipers getting faster. All was going well until we got to the mid-section where the edge of the road is marked by snow poles just to let you know just how close you are to being deep in the shit. Suddenly I saw one very large set of lights from a truck coming towards me. As I prepared for the passing spray a second set of lights appeared. Some lunatic was attempting to overtake and there was no way he was going to make it. The guy in the truck let him know what he thought by blasting on his horn. He kept coming and then he began to weave across the road. He was heading right for me and there was nowhere I could go. I daren't touch the breaks so I just eased my car to the edge of the road and braced myself. At the last moment the lunatic swerved across the road and slid down the side of my car taking the wing mirror clean off. As I eased my car down to a stop he just kept on going. The guy in the truck blasted him all the way down the road. As I sat there the guys in the cars behind came up to see if I was alright. I assured them I was ok and quickly checked the car. The damage was all bodywork so I continued on to Blackpool. When I arrived at the Gables Hotel the guys in the bar poured out to check on me. I checked in and called home. "How was the journey?" asked Jayne. "Uneventful," I reply. I'd let her know what happened tomorrow. Right now I was going to finish the beer in front of me and hit the scratcher as I had an early check-in the day after.

THURSDAY FEBRUARY 9TH

I get to the heliport just after 6.00am for a 6.30am check-in. I hand the battered car into Hertz and sign the usual accident form. I grab a paper and a cup of tea and soon afterwards my flight gets called. It's the usual procedure. You show your ID badge and then you and your kit bag gets a full security search. You are then given a survival suit and a life jacket. The suit is a waterproof all-in-one with elasticated neck and arm seals. The life jacket is just a harnessed clip on. You then have to watch a safety brief for the type of chopper you are going to use for the fifteen-minute flight to the platform. In the North Sea you use Tigers and Super Pumas but here it's a ten-seated Dolphin. The formation is 3-4-3 so the lads in the know either line up 1-2-3 or 7-8-9-10. Some of them just don't want to go in at 4-5-6 as that means you get to sit in the cramped three seats in the back row. I have never given it much thought really. If we hit the sea like a dart then it isn't going to make much difference either way. Sure enough I'm in the back row.

We were half-way through the flight and I was still thinking about what I was going to say to Jayne about the near-miss when our pilot pulled back on the stick. The chopper went into a controlled hover and we just sat there. The pilot then turns to us, points to his eyes and then out through the front window. We all look on. All of a sudden this military jet screams across our path. By the time we hear the bang it's gone. Calm as you like the pilot sets off once more. After landing on the helideck and shaking hands with my btb Mick, I hand him the paper and wish him well on his leave. At check-in we were told that when the RAF are using the area, all the offshore installations would get a last minute warning so that no alarm bells go off. Right now I envy those people that just have to get the bus to work.

Friday February 10th

In addition to being allocated a bunk when you arrive offshore you are given a t-card. This carries your name, bunk number and associated lifeboat. One of first duties is to find the lifeboat concerned and place your card in it. If ever the platform alarms go off in earnest or because of a drill then you stop what you are doing, make your workplace safe, go to the lifeboat and turn your card. There is a muster checker there to help you if you can't remember your name or you have forgotten how to count. Now if you are on a bridge-linked installation then you get a second card for the racks situated at the bridge of the vessel you are on. It's a simple system whereby if you go across the bridge you move your card accordingly and when you return you do the reverse. This also lets people know where you are and helps the drills and platform clearances required when radiography is taking place.

The construction guys on the tools offshore are collectively known as 'The Bears'. It's an apt term and every morning at the bridge t-card racks, there are plenty of lumbering sore-headed ones. Now let's jump forward to lunchtime and shift completion. Those bears then turn into fleeing wildebeest. As they stampede across the bridge it's a very brave man that attempts to go the other way. Once at the racks it becomes every man for himself. Cards are snatched and dumped and the race continues onto the galley. Some guys even mark their cards in such a way that they are easily recognisable. You see big red dots, black squares, stripes and all kinds of wavy patterns. The system works but when someone like Trevor has rifled the stationery cupboard then you know there is going to be trouble. I have seen many a riot break out because the board has now got twenty big red dots, fifteen black squares and no end of modified patterns.

SATURDAY FEBRUARY 11TH

After an exhausting sixteen-hour day of wading through mechanical completion documentation I have been informed that I have won the football coupon. It's £5 a go and you have to guess home, away or draw for twenty listed football matches. God only knows how I managed to get sixteen of them right but that's just what I did. As is tradition I go to the bonded store and get the cokes, chocolate, fags and cigars in and put them in the tea shack. A quick shower is followed by a night in the TV lounge. As I ponder on what good deed I can do with some of the money the pre-film adverts give me three choices. I could either send some money to Mary in Africa so that she won't have to walk three miles each morning to get clean water, I could send some money to a group in Belgium so that bears won't have to dance for tourists anymore or I could pay most of it to my gas supplier so that they could service my boiler each year. As the movie credits suddenly appear I make a decision. Mary can move closer to the water and who needs a boiler in summer anyway. I'll send the bear some money.

SUNDAY FEBRUARY 12TH

Sunday again, and it's all about progress reports. Not one of the best ways to spend a Sunday. Take three weeks ago today for instance. Back then I awoke with the words 'Carpe diem' ringing in my ears. Something or somebody was telling me to seize the day. The last time it happened was on the final day of a family holiday in Las Vegas. We had a few hours to burn before getting the flight and although everyone had loved it they just wanted to be going home. "Carpe diem," I said to the kids. "You never know, this morning you could meet the most interesting person of the holiday." We were in the Bellagio and just across the strip was the Paris Las Vegas Hotel. We wandered around it for a few hours and then went up its tower. The elevator attendant at the top was a charming old man by the name of Michael. My son asked him about Vegas and then he began to tell him about the thirty years he had worked there. Pretty soon he had an audience. Michael had met all the great names when he spent a decade at Caesar's Palace and since then he had seen many changes over the years. The one story that stuck with me was to do with Sammy Davis Jr. After doing shows in Caesar's he was never allowed to leave by the front door because of the colour of his skin. When Frank Sinatra began to play there and found out about it he said that he would only leave by the same door as Sammy. The idiotic rule was dropped and both entertainers proudly left by the front. As we left, my son Matthew gave Michael fifty dollars and thanked him. His face lit up. "Carpe diem," said Matthew. "Carpe diem."

I was in two minds whether or not to go to church. "Carpe diem," says the voice in my head. I get up and go. Fifteen minutes into the mass and we are introduced to four missionaries from Africa. Their dark skins are wrapped in the bright colours of the rainbow. The leader is called Moses and he steps forward to tell us all just what God means to him. He then breaks into song. Moments later four soulful voices fill the church. The hairs on the back of my neck stood on end. I left that church two feet taller than I had went in. You see, you just never know.

Progress reports my arse.

MONDAY FEBRUARY 13TH

Whenever a fellow Teessider joins the team offshore the last thing you want is for him to look like a buffoon on his first day. Well today a planner called Ken did just that. As I walked down towards the TV lounge a line of guys passed me, laughing their heads off. When I get to the washbasin area just before the lounge I see why. Ken is standing there with a towel around his waist. The top half of his body is covered in foam and the water is everywhere. When I ask him just what the hell he's doing he tells me that his room is rubbish. It's got nowhere to wash, no toilet and no shower. When I ask him to show me his room I walk in and pull on a handle sticking out from one of the walls. Lo and behold it opens up to all the things on his list. Sometimes offshore you meet them and I'm sure it's not going to be the last time I will have to explain something to him. On second thoughts they do say that you can't educate pork, don't they?

TUESDAY FEBRUARY 14TH

Offshore Fire and Gas (F&G) systems are there for detection and protection. The detection side consists of various types of detectors arranged to monitor all the areas where a fire or hydrocarbon/toxic gas release may occur. The protection system initiates shutdown actions, releases fixed fire fighting systems and alerts personnel based on hazard information it has identified. Basically they are designed to ensure that the consequences of a fire or abnormal gas escape are minimised for the safety and protection of people, plant and the environment. So when faults and spurious alarms occur they need to be sorted quickly. Rob, our instrument commissioning engineer, got in touch with me today to say that he was sending over someone to go through the as-built documentation we had on the system. When I asked for a name all I got was "The Sniper's Dream." He was still laughing as he put the phone down. For the next hour or so I dealt with everyone that entered the office and then he appeared. There was no introduction necessary as this guy had the biggest head I have ever seen on a human being. The shadow it cast on the wall was frightening. The name "The Sniper's Dream" was perfect as there was no way you could miss it at a few thousand yards with a high-powered rifle.

WEDNESDAY FEBRUARY 15TH

Xerox copiers the world over always fall over now and then and it takes one of those strange creatures from the supplier to fix them. Now that's an easy task when the damn things are onshore in an office somewhere but it's slightly different when they are offshore. That means flying one of the poor souls out to the platform and obviously they don't like that much. A few of our copiers are in need of a service so a young lad called Vince arrives on-board to sort them. He is terrified of heights, not too keen on the water and according to him all the machines are full of gremlins. Needless to say he thought that he might have to stay the night. That ended the moment roustabout Mark kissed him on the cheek and told him that he was looking forward to seeing his ass. I have never seen anyone work so hard and those gremlins just seemed to disappear without a trace.

We all had a deep and meaningful discussion at the end of the evening meeting. It was over a point of concern and I'm glad to say it was dealt with in a professional manner. Oink was going to try and stop saying 'oink' anymore and he needed a word to replace it. The marker board on the wall that was covered in some nonsense about the cooling medium system got wiped. Thirty brainstorming minutes later we came up with the word 'zig'. He liked it and was going to give it a try.

THURSDAY FEBRUARY 16TH

The weather is getting up. Visibility isn't that good in the field. As for new boy Ken I had guessed right. I'm at the bridge and he approaches me like a gorilla. He's looking down at the floor and seems to be having a problem standing upright. When I ask him what's wrong he just says that he can't get used to sleeping with his life jacket on. Apparently the lad in his room did it and said it was a safety requirement just in case the alarm went off when they were asleep. Once the lights were out said roommate took his off. I'm sure now that when the good lord gave us all heads Ken thought he must have had said sheds and asked for a big empty one.

On a brighter note, when I was at home I got a signed Manchester United shirt off eBay and passed it to the charity committee. All the tickets were sold and the shirt was won by one of our material controllers. The lads have helped a good cause to the tune of £500.

FRIDAY FEBRUARY 17TH

If there is one thing that no offshore worker wants to hear first thing in the morning it's the foghorn. This morning that's what greets me. Managers on board immediately start thinking about how it will impact on their current schedules. When will the boats be able to deliver the materials we need? When will the choppers bring the vendors we have been waiting for? At my level you just spare a thought for those lads that have completed a trip and just want to go home. Some lads will wind them up about it but it's something I have never done and never will.

A mass meeting was called and then we are all told something else we certainly didn't want to hear. Jimmy, our piping engineer, had died. The previous night he had gone to see the medic about what felt like indigestion. He was given some tablets and then informed that he would be checked on during the night. His lifeless body was found around 3.00am. A heart attack was mentioned. Due to the fog he couldn't be moved so they took him to the clinic. The whole platform felt numb all day. Some went to their rooms for the duration while others quietly did some work. A collection was organised and in addition arrangements were made for a card and some flowers.

Jimmy was a lovely little fella – always smiling and cracking a joke. He really was one of those people that loved life no matter where it took him and that's not easily said in this industry. I said a prayer for him.

SATURDAY FEBRUARY 18TH

The two most common rates for contractors in this game are 'the hourly rate' and 'the day rate'. The hourly rate does what it says on the tin in that you get paid for every hour on your timesheet. The day rate is just an agreed rate per day regardless of the hours you work. Both have their pros and cons and so it's just down to the individual preference really. I always remember the time when I was working offshore in the North Sea and the company I was with were transferring from one to the other and it caused all kinds wars. When everyone was on an hourly rate the lads who lived local always wanted to be offshore on the first flights out. Two weeks later at the end of a trip they wanted to be on the last ones in. The travelling lads wanted to go offshore on the last flights and come in on the first ones. The local lads were in no rush and earned more money and the travelling lads gained with time so everyone was happy. When everyone was put on a day rate the manoeuvring started. The local lads now wanted to go offshore on the last flights and come in on the first ones. The travelling lads would then lose it big style. The firm I was working for had its own little royal family who thought that they could get away with anything, and with a twisted company rep for backing, they usually did.

The weather cleared long enough to get a chopper out to take Jimmy back in.

Sunday February 19TH

Today I took a moment off from the progress reports and thought back to my last Sunday at home. It all had to do with a little verse on maths. "Remember tonight when you run for the bus a minus a minus equals a plus." My old deputy head master, Christopher Laird, used to have plenty of lines like that. He taught me maths, was a disciplinarian and was well respected by all pupils that went through St. Patrick's School in Thornaby-on-Tees. I have so much to thank him for. I was one of his pupils and he taught me a lot. As I left church there was a tap on my shoulder. He was standing there with a group of friends. "This is one of my lads," he announces to them. "Hello Andrew, are you ok?"

"Hello sir," I reply. "Yes I'm fine."

"How's it going on the oil rigs?" he asks. He then stepped back as I talked about what we were doing to get the oil and gas out from under the sea. The people with him stood open-mouthed and he just watched them and me with pride on his face. As we shook hands and said our goodbyes he leant into me and whispered, "You can call me Chris you know."

"I can't you know," I replied. "Take care, sir." He smiled and nodded, he knew exactly what I meant.

Monday February 20TH

Today I listened to one of the best safety talks I have ever heard. We had gathered in the cinema for the usual boring brief when Willie, the safety rep, stepped before the big screen. Moments later a picture of his family appeared on it. "What do you see?" he asked. Well as you can imagine all kinds of abuse and nonsense was hurled at him. When it eventually stopped he asked the same question once more. This time words like 'wife', 'son', 'daughter', 'family', 'love', 'togetherness' and 'bond' were used. Willie then stepped a little closer.

"It's late, you're tired, you're cold and you have one last job to do on the mezz deck before getting indoors to for a shower, a good feed and that movie you have been waiting to see. You get it sorted and on your way in you see some material that hasn't been secured properly. Not my problem, you say, and off you go. The shower felt great, the food was good and you were just about to enter the cinema when you hear the news. Willie has had an accident. He was on his way in from the cellar deck when he was struck by some lose objects that had dropped from the mezz deck. The medic is in attendance and a helicopter has been scrambled. Later on you hear that I died on the way to the hospital.

"Picture the two policemen at my door as they break the news to my widow. Picture the faces of my children as they learn that Daddy isn't coming home anymore. Think about the loss, not just the human side but also the financial side. Three lives have just been turned upside down. Yes the tears will eventually stop, yes they will survive and life will go on but what about all the moments that have gone forever and, what about me? I don't get to share in their joy or wipe away their tears. I don't get to see them grow up. I don't see their first hangover or that magic moment when they pass their driving test and get a car. I don't get to walk my daughter down the aisle or see my son go through honourable manhood. I don't get any more moments with the woman I have loved since we first met at school.

"Think again, you are at the door to the accommodation, you want to go in but something is bothering you. Those lose objects are preying on your mind. You close the door and come looking for me. You find me, show me the problem and together we make it safe. Later than expected we both set off back in. When we get to the accommodation we meet Trevor in the locker room. "All right mate?" you ask. "No," he bleats. "There is no hot water, the food was crap and the movie was a bag of shite.

"Now then, promise me you are going to look out for me. Promise me that when you see something not quite right you are going to take time to correct it. Promise me that no matter what, you are always going to put safety first, just promise me."

Every single person in the cinema did just that.

TUESDAY FEBRUARY 21ST

A guy in a suit walked into the office today and introduced himself as Nigel, the auditor. He said that he and his team were here to see if we were following the agreed handover procedures. It was news to me; normally I got notified and go over the guidelines, etc. Anyway he plonks himself down and starts firing the questions. After about thirty minutes of interrogations Zig walked in. He comes over to the desk and I switch the tape to record. "Go on then, John," I say. "Let's hear a megazig." He puts his hand on the shoulder of the auditor and leans into the tape and screams "Zig zig zigardee zig zig zigardee zig zig zigardee zigardee zigardee ZIGARDEEEEEEEEEEEEEE, oh fuck it, ooooooooooooooooooooooooooink." I stopped the tape and everyone in the office belly laughed. Nigel, the auditor, closed his book and quietly left. I didn't care, we had Oink back. I waited for him to leave before rewinding the tape. Now, offshore anyone can make a tannoy announcement. All you have to do is press one-five-nine, wait for the tone and speak. So I hit the keys, waited for the tone and then pressed play on the tape. That's when everyone on the platform heard the megazig. Moments later the Offshore Installation Manager came on the same tannoy and asked John to report to this office immediately. Talk yourself out of that one, I thought.

WEDNESDAY FEBRUARY 22ND

Well that's another trip done and as I settle down on the top bunk with a cup of tea and the diary, my roommate Barry says something that gets my attention. "You know son I enjoy my last night offshore more than my last night at home." I was going to say something but then I realised what he had just said. The last night at home always has you on a little downer as you know pretty soon you are going to say goodbye to the ones you love. The last night offshore has you on the up as you know you have safely come through another trip and now you are going home to your family for two weeks. We talk about our children but in particular our young sons. We are well aware of the importance in spending as much time as possible with them and we don't need reminding of it. That said every now and then something comes along that does just that. Barry hands me a tape and points to a song called *Cats in the Cradle* by Harry Chapin. I switch on my Sony Walkman and switch off the light. A few minutes later I am in tears. It's a story of a father not making time for his son and when his son grows up he ends up doing the same to his father. I just hope it's a trap I never fall into.

THURSDAY FEBRUARY 23RD

We all have our little routines and when I head home from offshore one of mine always involves Chris Rea. People do say to you that it must be great to open your front door and realise that you are home. Well for me it's a bit earlier than that. On the drive home I play all kinds of music until I see the Teesside skyline. That's when the music of local musician Chris Rea is put on and the volume is turned up a notch. That's when I start to relax, that's when that little voice in my head says, "You're home now, son." That's when Chris reminds me.

I was born and raised on steel river
I see it all like it was yesterday
The ships and bridges they were all delivered
From Sydney harbour to the Cisco bay.

TRIP THREE

Big John, our welding inspector, has had to go into see the doctor in the base at Barrow-in-Furness because his little con-trick has backfired. He had put in a claim for industrial deafness so they have made him undergo a full set of tests. So for me it's a quiet night. That idea gets put on hold as soon as I leave the hotel restaurant and Rolf and Billy are sitting at the bar. Rolf is a German commissioning engineer who can't say a single sentence without getting animated. Billy is a telecoms engineer who has a stammer. And no, I am not making it up. Anyway, they order me a drink and I make a call home. Back at the bar they ask if everything is ok. "Not really," I say. "I was on the phone for five minutes and must have said all of three words." Rolf shakes his head. "I called my wife from the phone in my room. What is wrong with this damn country? The connection was useless, the sound was awful and it took me ten minutes just to say hello." Billy just gives us both one of those looks.

"Yyyyyyyy…yyyyyyyy…yuuuuuor…luuuucky…………." he began. "It takkkkkkkkkeeeeeessssss…mmmmmmmmm…mmmmm…mmmmmyyyyyyyyyyy wwwwife ffff…ffffffff…ffffifteeen mmmmmm…mmmmm…minutes before she knows it's me cccccccalling." I get to bed several laughs and just as many beers later.

THURSDAY MARCH 8TH

After going through the handover notes I spent the afternoon with Bobby, the painting inspector. We had some structural area clearances to go over and the monotony of it all was broken by one of Bobby's stories. During his leave he went out with the wife for an Indian and a few beers and then spent the rest of the night with his head down the toilet. A doctor was called and to Bobby's dismay he was from India. Now, Indian food, yes, but Indian doctors, well that just got a big 'no'.

Straight away the blood pressure is on the up as Bob has to endure a barrage of questions. The doctor wanted to know about his diet and then made him rattle off everything he had eaten in the previous forty-eight hours. Eventually Bob got to the Indian meal. The doctor listened and then asked, "Did you have any black stools?"

"No," replied Bob.

"Are you sure?" replied the doctor.

"They weren't on the menu," says Bob.

"I mean when you got home," says the doctor.

"No, we finished everything on the plate and besides I never ask for left-overs to be put in doggy bags." As you can imagine the doctor got more exasperated by the minute and in the end Bobby just exploded and threw him out of the house. It wasn't until his wife explained that the doctor was trying to find out what he was crapping did Bob crumble with embarrassment.

FRIDAY MARCH 9TH

Sometimes with the comms links out here it's like being in the dark ages. When they go down, and at times it can be quite frustrating, the only way to call home is by using the phone in the radio room. Well as you can imagine you end up talking over each other and if that's not bad enough, Norman the platform radio operator is a right nosey sod. You could be having a conversation with the wife and when you put the phone down he will start asking you about something you mentioned. "I bought one of them and mine's the same," he would say. You would look blank and then he would go on about the car you had just been talking about. You can tell him to mind his own business but it just gets lost somewhere in that thick skin of his.

You have to book a ten-minute slot for the phone and today I was behind Gary, one of the insulators. Gary is right into his martial arts and doing the job he does he gets known as 'Enter the lagging. Bruce Lee, eat your bloody heart out'. Anyway Gary is just about to finish his call slightly early and Norman is listening in as usual. He nods and winks and lets his wife terminate the call before he starts. "What do you mean you have something to tell me? What for God's sake? A what? You've gone and got another tattoo? Where this time? On your arse, an eagle, how big is it? How big? That means it must just be about touching that snake that runs down your back. You've gone too far this time, girl. I was just about getting used to those pigs heads you had done around your nipples. You just wait until I get home." After that he slammed the phone down and stormed out of the room.

Norman almost exploded. I told him that I had met Gary's wife and she was an absolute barn pot when she'd had a drink. He wanted to go into the details but I had a call to make. I think it was the only time he never asked me anything about it when it was over.

SATURDAY MARCH 10TH

At home a Christmas tree is something that is taken out of the loft each December so that it can be decorated with lights and presents. Well when you are offshore a Christmas tree is an assembly of spools, valves and fittings, the primary function of which is to control the flow of oil or gas out of a well. Its other functions range from water and gas injection to enhance production rates to well intervention, pressure relief and monitoring means. It's called a Christmas tree because of its crude resemblance to the yuletide ornament, but the difference in price is immense. So when a few of them start playing up and it looks like a trend has appeared the suppliers send their boffins out. The problem with that is at the moment we are on a full POB (Persons On Board) and none of the project teams are prepared to give up any of their allocated bed spaces, even if it is only for a few days. Shuttling is out of the question at the moment as the flight plans are full and besides the down time and expense involved have to be taken into account. The only option left is for the crew that comes on to 'hotbed' with existing teams' crews. Hot bedding offshore isn't liked by anyone but sometimes it has to be used and it works as follows. When the selected dayshift members get up for work their bed sheets get changed immediately by the catering crew. The hot bedders, who have worked the night shift then climb in. When they go on shift the same happens with the sheets. People don't like the inconvenience of additional gear in their rooms or the fact that they have to keep out while others are in but there is a plus point. There is an additional allowance payable for the inconvenience so the greedy and needy tend not to complain too much.

SUNDAY MARCH 11TH

A few Sundays ago I was listening to a sermon on the paradox of life. According to it we have taller buildings but shorter tempers. We have wider roads but narrower viewpoints. We've got bigger houses but smaller families, more conveniences but less time, more knowledge and less judgement, more experts and yet more problems. We have multiplied our possessions but reduced our values and loved too little yet hated too often. We've managed to add years to our lives but not life to our years and we know how to make a living but not a life. We have been to the moon and back and still have trouble crossing the street. We've cleaned the air and polluted the soul, conquered the atom but not prejudice, we write more and learn less and we've learnt how to rush but not how to wait.

So by all accounts these are times of fast food and slow digestion, big men and small characters, steep profits and shallow relationships, fixed incomes and broken homes. As I sit on my bunk and contemplate the enormity of it all I just wish someone would invent a happy pill and then all this wouldn't really matter would it. I mean we've got pills for just about everything else haven't we?

MONDAY MARCH 12TH

At this morning's meeting Paul, our scaffolding foreman, was put on the spot about an altercation that had taken place in the early hours of the morning. A pipe spool that had been welded during the night had deliberately been positioned through the rungs of a twenty-foot ladder. That meant that the ladder had to be cut in half to make two ten-foot ones. At the moment twenty-foot ladders are like gold dust as some squads cut them into four sections so that they can use them for access in tight areas. So as you can imagine the scaffs are getting a bit narked with it all. Anyway a pipe fitter and a scaff almost came to blows over said incident and if it wasn't for a couple of roaming safety reps things could have got out of hand. As Paul sat sunken-shouldered in his seat he made an apology on behalf of his team; he ended it with one of the best lines I have ever heard in such a forum. He just sighed and said, "It's absferfuckinglutely posserfuckingtively saborfuckingtage."

TUESDAY MARCH 13TH

I went to see old Joe today, the tech clerk for the welding inspectors. Heaven knows how he ever passed the offshore medical. For a start he is stone deaf. Every time you approach him and ask him a question you always get a, "Say again, son" after which you have to repeat the question again. It's that barmy that now people just go up to him and say things like "Joe, wobarty wob wob wobarty."

"Say again, son."

"Have you got the radiographs they did last night?"

Today he asked me to do him a favour. He handed me an old set of coloured Stabilo pens which had the actual colours written down the stem of each one. He then handed me a new set that were blank and asked me to write the colours on them. During all the whispering he confided in me that although he was colour blind he had to mark the status of the offshore welds on the isometrics in accordance with an agreed colour code. Yellow meant the joint had been prepared, blue meant that it had been welded, pink, orange and green covered the magnetic particle, ultrasonic and radiographic non-destructive testing carried out on each weld. If there was a weld repair found then red was used. He didn't want it to be common knowledge that he was colour blind so he never asked the inspectors to do it for him. His mate Terry was on leave and he usually did it so I was asked to step in. I did it and promised not to mention it to anyone. Anyway so Joe is not only deaf, he is colour blind. I'm sure it doesn't stop there.

WEDNESDAY MARCH 14TH

A very famous woman once wrote, *Life is an opportunity, benefit from it. Life is beauty, admire it. Life is a dream, realise it. Life is a challenge, meet it. Life is a duty, complete it. Life is a game, play it. Life is costly, care for it. Life is wealth, keep it. Life is love, enjoy it. Life is a mystery, know it. Life is a promise, fulfil it. Life is sorrow, overcome it. Life is a song, sing it. Life is a struggle, accept it. Life is a tragedy, comfort it. Life is an adventure, dare it. Life is luck, make it. Life is too precious, do not destroy it. Life is life, fight for it.* That woman was Mother Teresa. Well today 'Life' for me had 'Boat' strapped on the end of it. We had a spurious alarm on the platform and so as per procedure we all mustered at the lifeboats. We remained there for about ninety minutes because some boats had more souls than they should have. When the checkers called it in, the investigation began. Blame was shared and people were eventually educated and then moved. Amongst it all was a card for someone that had left the platform yesterday. HSE were going to have a field day.

THURSDAY MARCH 15TH

It was a PR day today as a film crew and a team of local reporters have arrived on board to give the inhabitants of Lancashire an insight into what we are doing. The visit was all cloak and dagger stuff and the management were on a need-to-know basis. They did get full of themselves at times. Anyway, as they were escorted all over the place, the cameras rolled and the pens noted it all down. The one thing that struck me about it was that these people were reacting to things I just took for granted. They walked across grating and watched the sea explode beneath their feet and cawed like little children. When a dummy was thrown into the water and the zodiac that was scrambled from a project standby vessel got to it in less than two minutes they clapped with joy. They were in awe of Archie, the crane driver, as he was dropping containers on a sixpence of a supply boat as it rolled around the waves. They just couldn't believe the relaxed manner in which the team on that boat moved the containers into position before carrying out transfers to the platform. Their minds boggled as they stood in the control room and watched the operators control various functions on the platform from their consoles. It's only when you see this reaction do you remember just what professional people are around you. These people are special. They don't act it, they don't ask for recognition of it, they don't seek it, they just are.

FRIDAY MARCH 16TH

Whenever you hear the term 'OWL' offshore it's not often the bird variety. OWL offshore are 'Outstanding Work Lists.' Basically they are known incomplete scopes of work. Well not today they aren't because we have a short-eared one on the platform. Over the last few days the lads have been reporting bundles of feathers all over the place and today we found out why. A short eared owl has taken up residence so that it can pick off all the migrating birds that drop in for a rest. This fella is quite prolific and he is something to look at. Our presence doesn't seem to bother him at all and to be honest I think he quite likes the celebrity status he has obtained here. On top of that he can fly off here and go to the beach whenever he wants to.

I slipped into the welding inspector's office at lunchtime and swapped old Joe's Stabilo pens out with ones I had mixed the colours on. Yellow Stabilo has blue written on it, blue Stabilo has yellow written on it, etc.

SATURDAY MARCH 17TH

Some of the lads have been working a ghoster on the emergency power systems and it's helped enormously in getting the thing up and running. A ghoster offshore is simply a term for someone who doesn't go to bed at the end of a shift, they work right through instead. It makes for a hard twenty-four hour period and it's not something HSE departments like. Anyway the job got done and the big chiefs are happy once more.

There is hell going on in the welding office. Several isometrics are a mess and senior inspector Jimmy is having a fit over it. Old Joe is wandering around in a state of shock.

I was handed a local news rag today and I read two of the reports from the team that was out here. It sounded like they were little kids given sole access to a big toy store. I am sure it will make fascinating reading to some but as I thought the guys out here don't recognise it.

SUNDAY MARCH 18TH

It was one hell of a boring progress meeting today. The brick counters just went on and on. They should have taken a leaf out of the book of my parish priest. A few weeks ago he got to his feet, walked to the pulpit and said "An argument for brevity. The Lord's Prayer is 66 words, the Gettysburg Address is 286 words and the Declaration of Independence is 1322 words." After a brief pause he then said, "The United States of America has just issued its governmental regulation review on the sale of cabbage – it runs to 26, 911 words." As we all began to smile, he then said, "I am having dinner with the Bishop so when we discussed my sermon today he just asked me to be informative, be funny, and be seated." When he did so the whole church laughed its way into the next hymn.

I slipped back into the welding inspector's office and swapped the Stabilos. Old Joe has gone to see the medic.

Monday March 19th

If you are the type of person that can't get off to sleep because some little noise was irritating you or some small spec of light was finding its way to you then this industry will clear you of all that. You could end up sharing a room with someone that snores little a pissed rhinoceros or your bedroom wall could be all that comes between you and those very polite, unassuming, quiet drillers. You may even end up sleeping on an overcrowded platform that is way behind schedule and so every shift pattern known to man is in place with little time for thought about much else. Whatever it is, after a few trips you learn to sleep through hurricanes, earthquakes and world wars. Space and silence is important to all offshore workers and so they tend to be very tolerant people because quite simply they don't have a choice in not getting any. Most of them have mastered the trick of shutting their systems down even when they are surrounded by all kinds of crap. They take what space is given and find a way to fill it with what silence they can. So the next time you are in the middle of some incredibly noisy situation and you come across someone who is either not to fussed or purring like a cat, he probably works offshore.

Tuesday March 20th

Creatures of habit; Yes I know we are but some habits are a bit odd. One of mechanical boys called Tony left the office tonight and said he was going for a shower and a practice pack. I met him later in the TV lounge and asked about the practice pack bit. He goes home on the same day as me and he said that although the last night is his pack night, the night before that is his practice pack night. He actually goes and puts his gear into his bag and then takes it out again. I'm sure there is a medical term for it.

Wednesday March 21st

Today is all about timesheets and expenses. We have to get ours approved by the OIM (Offshore Installation Manager) and sometimes he can bit chewy with the expenses bit. Its micro management and it's a bit of a joke really. Mine are usually straightforward but in our office is a jock document controller called Brian and his never are. He lives up in the highlands and so his journeys are always trains, planes and automobiles. Sure enough he has had his rejected because of some meal he had claimed for. He stared at it for a while just so that his blood could boil over. His timing was perfect. Just as he was about to go off the OIM appeared in our office doorway. "You know something. That old twat never rapes you. Oh no not him, for him you have to drop your pants, open the cheeks of your arse and welcome the bastard in." We all watched in silence as the OIM quietly walked away.

THURSDAY MARCH 22ND

The wind is up and although that helps choppers it sometimes doesn't help you when you are walking across a helideck towards a chopper with the blades still spinning. On deck there is a collapsible handrail and in such cases it's put upright and a rope gets attached to it and to the chopper. Today they don't see any need for the rope. The chopper managed to jerk its way onto the deck and the lads coming on-board struggled their way towards us. One guy fell over and began to panic. Next thing we see a newspaper and what looked like a wallet tumble across the deck. He's now clinging onto the netted rope and so the HLO (Helideck Landing Officer) and his crew have to bundle him to safety. Believe me it's not the best advert before embarking on a chopper but hey I'm going home and if the pilot is alright with it then so am I. After a bumpy ride in and a careful drive home I get a call from Mick to see if all went well. He tells me that the panic merchant who was a new start for operations had lost it and he's under watch from the medic. The episode had frightened him so much that he has resigned and wants off the platform as soon as the weather improves.

TRIP FOUR

WEDNESDAY APRIL 4TH

I had to set off early as my offshore medical had run out and so it was off to the company-approved quack in Barrow-in-Furness. I met Steve, one of the QA lads, there. He was a bit nervous as he's a very big lad and was no stranger to the dessert trolley. Anyway, eventually this chain-smoking stick insect in a white coat coughed his way over to us. Looking up from the folder flapping between his bony fingers, "Steve," he croaked. "Yes, I'm Steve," says big lad.

"Oh dear," began the doc. "You are a sorry looking fat boy, aren't you?" Steve went red and I did as best I could to hold a laugh in. "I don't eat that much," lied Steve.

"So what's your excuse?" enquired the quack. "Is someone force feeding you while you are asleep?" I almost fell over. Steve never saw the funny side and quietly followed him to an inspection room. I got a lovely efficient doctor called Karen. She checked me against the required UKOOA (United Kingdom Offshore Operators Association) regulations. Urine and blood samples were sent to the labs and she checked the senses, organs and limbs. An ECG and X-ray later I was given the thumbs up. Steve was told to diet. Apparently his quack had told him that although he only had one arse he was eating like he had two.

The evening in Blackpool was a quiet one. I had pasta and a few pints and that was me. Steve had half a cow and a Diet Coke. Big John was getting in late so I wouldn't see him until morning.

THURSDAY APRIL 5TH

The Gables Hotel was in chaos this morning. The whole lobby area had been flooded. It was something to do with a leaking shower in Big John's room. My arse, I thought and got the real reason out of him at the heliport. He got in that late he just had time to grab a dozen small cans of beer. He drank six and put the other six in his sink. The plug was in and the cold water tap was on. It just ran into the overflow and so John thought he could have six chilled ones for breakfast. The only problem was that the overflow connection had split and so the water had gone everywhere. When they rang his room he quickly moved the cans and switched his shower to drip mode. The guy that knocked on the door fell for it. It's a good job we don't get breathalysed on a regular basis.

FRIDAY APRIL 6TH

On average around three thousand people are killed or seriously injured each year in drink-drive collisions on UK roads. Nearly one in six of all deaths on the road involve drivers who are over the legal alcohol limit of eighty milligrams in one hundred millilitres. The reason I know this is that Willie, the safety rep, gave us another reminder in his presentation today. He does have a way with words and the last time I heard a drink-drive speech it was from my local priest but he had an extra spin in his story.

"She refused to speak to anyone so the nuns just called her Angel. She had been brought to them after both of her parents had been run over and killed by a drunken driver. The local villages couldn't shed any light on their identity as they were not local to the area. Sister Sarah was given the task of trying to connect with the child. After a few days that had brought nothing more than nods and brief smiles, it was time for a new approach. Sarah took her to a bible class that was being run by Sister Mary and attended by a local group of six-year old children. Mary was aware of the orphaned child's plight and so sat her at the back of the class. Sister Sarah left the room and waited by the open door. Sister Mary began the lesson. She opened a book and turned to a page that contained a picture of Jesus Christ. She held it up for all to see and asked the class if anyone knew the man in the picture. The class remained quiet. After a few moments everyone heard a chair scrape across the floor and turned to see Angel standing. 'I know who he is', she said. 'That was the man that held me in his arms the night my mother and father died."

SATURDAY APRIL 7TH

What is the longest horse race in the flat season? Well the answer to that is being run today and it's the Grand National. Yes, it's over jumps but it's in the flat season. Anyway, it's sweep time and so I have handed over my money and got some nag that should be called Notacatinhellschance. I was then reminded by the gambling crew that as the British Horse Racing Authority computer only has room for eighteen characters no horse can have a name longer than that. I am then duly informed that is why some horses have all the letters of their name together as spaces count. Top tipster Eddie from logistics then tells us of the naughty names that people have tried to get past the governing body. These gems include; Arfur Foulkesaycke, OilBeefHooked, Hugh G Dildeaux, Norfolk Enchants, Hoof Hearted, Pee Nesenvy, Ivanna Threesome, Jack Schitt, Wear The Fox Hat, Sofa Can Fast and Are Soles To You. Anyway Notacatinhellschance or whatever its name fell at the sixth.

SUNDAY APRIL 8TH

A test separator is a vessel that receives wellhead fluids from any production wellhead via test manifolds. Production from each wellhead is periodically diverted from the high pressure and low pressure production manifolds to the test manifolds for evaluation and confirmation of flow conditions. These fluids are separated in the test separator into oil, water and gas streams. The flow and quality of each stream is measured and then the liquids are returned to the required separation and export system. Well this system was due for handover to operations today and we didn't have the best of starts. The bi-party punchlist walkdown between commissioning and operations uncovered a few anomalies and so the race was on. To answer some of them we needed certain vendor data and this was Sunday. Anyway, just when we thought we had hit a brick wall, calls were made, favours were done and as midnight approached, we managed to get it all together. The system was signed over and as I eventually crawled into my pit an old poem sprung to mind.

If you think you are beaten you are
If you think you dare not, you don't
If you like to win, but think that you can't
It's almost certain you won't
If you think you'll lose, you've lost
For out of the world we find
Success begins with a fellow's will
It's all in the state of mind
If you think you are outclassed, you are
You've got to think high to rise
You've got to be sure of yourself before
You can ever win a prize
Life's battles don't always go
To the stronger or faster man
But sooner or later the man who wins
Is the one who thinks that he can.

MONDAY APRIL 9TH

Everyone has their own little gym routine and I'm no different. I start with a run and then go onto free weights. There is a six-foot bearded stick insect that has started to use the offshore gym and he has a very strange routine. He comes in, picks up a free weight, holds it under his chin, squats to his knees and rises again. For the two previous forty-minute sessions I did, he just did that. Well today some of the lads couldn't hold it in any longer so they confronted him. He told them that he did it for his joints as he is a fell runner. Apparently he enjoys running up fells and mountains, etc. After a bit of light-hearted banter he challenged the lads to a test. Well that was it for me; I just stopped and watched as there was no going back for them now. Stick insect walked over to a free running machine, set it to high speed and tilted it up to its highest point. The first lad got on and lasted about a minute, the second lad was a lot less. Stick insect got on and calmly jogged for about five minutes before bringing the machine to a stop. When he quietly went back to his routine so did the rest of the room.

TUESDAY APRIL 10TH

How does a driller order four pints of beer? He usually does it by holding his entire right hand up. Drillers are renowned for losing fingers and roustabout

Terry is no different. While we were in the tea shack today he told us all how he lost the third finger on his right hand. He was climbing down off a pipe section and grabbed hold of some cable tray to steady himself. When he dropped to the deck his gloved hand snagged and he then felt a sharp pain. The glove on his hand turned red and he just thought he had cut his finger. When he removed the glove the section of finger that ran from his wedding ring remained inside. The finger was iced and when he eventually got to a hospital they told him that they could stitch it back on but it wouldn't be of much use. We often get told the dangers of wearing jewellery at work and Terry is a fine example of what can happen if you do.

WEDNESDAY APRIL 11TH

Roger, one of the quality assurance engineers, lives in Thailand, the place where you can get an Armani suit done in two hours for about fifty pence. So he thought he would have a bit of fun with the brigade that rubbishes every safety milestone gift we get. He has had a dozen t-shirts made with a nice picture of an oil rig neatly placed on the right breast section. Underneath that are the words "We're Safe, We're the 'A' team." At the morning meeting twelve people had them on and although strange looks were exchanged not a word was said. Word soon got around the platform that those people thought to be the hardest contributors to keeping everyone safe had received a t-shirt from the management. Now all we are talking about here is a two-bit sweat shop t-shirt that isn't going to last two washes in an offshore laundry. Well you should have seen the commotion it caused. Noses were seriously put out of joint and at the front of it all were the "What a load of shite" gang. Some guys were walking around with bottom lips like Volvo bumpers. I never realised such a little thing would affect some people so much. It got that bad even the people on the onshore base and in the London office were complaining that they had been left out once more. Hats off to Roger, for it turned out to be one hell of a wind up.

THURSDAY APRIL 12TH

The Breathing Air (BA) system is there to provide quality breathing air to various points on an offshore platform, including the recharging of air cylinders for personal BA apparatus, the recharging of lifeboat air cylinders and the distribution system throughout the topsides and drilling modules. Most of the day was spent on the final commissioning of the air compressor package so that we could get the system handed over to operations. Amongst all the high-speed dynamics of it all we got a visit from Bobby, our painting inspector. He waltzed into our office as if he didn't have a care in the world. The kettle went on and we asked Bob for a story. He told us a little gem about when he had just recently gone with his mates for a golfing weekend in Portugal. The hotel they stopped in was basic but Bob and his mates wanted it that way so that they could hit balls all day, get pissed all night and not offend anyone in the process. Anyway, day one went well for Bob. He had a great round of golf, some fine food and buckets full of beer. The problem started when he went back to his room for his first night of kip. The hotel he was in had two lifts. One was for personnel and the second was for goods and maintenance. The first one started on the first floor and went up to the fourteenth so the numbers on the buttons were simply one to fourteen. The second one started on the underground car park and its buttons were numbered one to fifteen. Bob was on floor eight and without thinking got into the second lift and pressed eight. The lift duly went to the floor below Bob's. He tried his key in the door and when it wouldn't work he used a phone in the corridor to ring reception. As he waited for someone to come up he took his shoes off and sat down by the door. He woke up three hours later busting for a piss. He gets the lift down to the lobby and goes to the toilet. He then gets back in the other lift and presses eight. He arrives at the right floor and sees that his shoes are no longer there. Thinking someone has stolen them he just sits down and goes back to sleep. When the maid woke him up a few hours later she wanted to know why he hadn't gone into his room. He hands her his room key and she puts it in the door and as if my magic it opened. With a puzzled look on his face he went in and had a shower. Minutes later there was a knock at the door and when he opened it he saw the maid from the floor below holding his shoes.

FRIDAY APRIL 13TH

When offshore inspections and tests are completed by the various disciplines, they complete what is known as an Inspection Test Record (ITR) or checksheet. These have all the details on the item in question and are full of tick boxes that have to be completed. At the bottom of each ITR there are signature boxes usually titled 'Completed By', 'Accepted By' and 'Approved By'. The guy that does the job signs the first box, his superior signs the second box and the third box is usually signed by some useless piece of space that has been issued with a stamp. Oink has got a stamp. It has got the project logo on it as well as the unique number that has been allocated to him. Some managers like that sort of thing. They love to have the number one under their name. Anyway John was number six until he decided to change things a little. He spent the whole morning cutting the padded section of his stamp away. He then sliced a rubber in half and outlined the word 'OINK' on it. He cut away the excess and then glued it into position. He then spent the whole afternoon with a red ink pad and pen hammering away at the ITRs that he had been forced to approve. It would never get noticed. Some documents out here have that many different stamps on them you would think they were the Magna Carta.

SATURDAY APRIL 14TH

B.B.B.B.B.B.Billy, our telecoms engineer, was trying to hand over the telephone system to operations today and they just about drove him mental in the end. As part of the handover his commissioning test procedure had a section for checking the extensions so Billy attempted to do that from the control room. Everyone had been informed and that's why everyone got into position and then at the last minute changed places. So as you can imagine Billy rings the correct extension of 2148 for the Operations Engineer and the Production Supervisor answers the phone with "2184 Tommy." This went on for about an hour and in between running around like a blue-arsed fly Billy almost cracked up. When he eventually worked it out he flew into the office and screamed, "You're just a bunch of cccccccccccccccccc clots." Yeah he had all of us going for a minute also.

SUNDAY APRIL 15TH

Who was responsible for murdering one quarter of the world's population? If you are thinking of Atilla the Hun, Idi Amin Dada, Pol Pot, Vlad the Impaler, Adolf Hitler or Josef Stalin, you would be wrong. The actual answer is Cain.

According to the book of Genesis, Cain and Abel were the two sons of Adam and Eve. Cain, the first-born was described as a crop farmer and Abel was a shepherd. Driven by jealousy, Cain committed the first murder by taking his younger brother out into a field and then killing him. So as there was only four people in the world at the time Cain reduced the population by one quarter.

It's a Sunday question and it was one of many that kept us entertained between progress reports and a lifeboat drill.

MONDAY APRIL 16TH

My roommate Barry had a cunning plan. As I am always up early and he can't get out of bed I bring him a cup of coffee. As he watches movies until late and I'm in bed either reading or writing, he would bring me a cup of tea. I duly did the coffee this morning and when he returned to the room tonight all the lights were out. He called my name a few times and then placed the drinks on the table. As he opened the adjoining door to the shared toilet, I stood up just as he was about to put the light on. His scream was deafening as was his fall to the floor. I lost count of how many knocks hit our door. As I chuckled away in my top bunk and Barry called me a twat for the one hundredth time he eventually just told me to read my sodding book. I gave him a verse from the poem *To the RAF* by Alfred Noyes.

> *Never since English ships went out*
> *To singe the beard of Spain,*
> *Or English sea-dogs hunted death*
> *Along the Spanish Main,*
> *Never since Drake and Raleigh won*
> *Our freedom of the seas,*
> *Have sons of Britain dared and done*
> *More valiantly than these.*

"Is there anymore?" he asked.
"Goodnight," I reply.
"Twat." Not exactly how the Waltons used to do it.

TUESDAY APRIL 17TH

Barry brings the tea and once more the lights are out. I'm a twat as usual and the search begins. He checks my bottom bunk, nothing. He then throws the toilet door open like something out of *Starsky and Hutch*, nothing. The room light is switched on and Barry removes his shirt. He then opens his wall locker and I take the shirt from him and say, "Thanks" before closing it again. I thought he was going to have a heart attack. People are banging on the walls and shouting abuse as he sits at the table hyperventilating. The twat issue is now at two hundred and I'm in the bunk. Eventually I give him a little bit of Byron and *Thy Days are Done*.

> *Thy days are done, thy fame begun;*
> *Thy country's strains record.*
> *The triumphs of her chosen son,*
> *The slaughter of his sword!*
> *The deeds he did, the fields he won,*
> *The freedom he restored!*

"Will I ever hear the full thing?" he asks.
"Night," I reply.
"Twat."

WEDNESDAY APRIL 18TH

Just a gerup and go now as we are off tomorrow. Barry brings the coffee to a darkened room. The lights go on straight away and doors are flung open. He then checks my bottom bunk, nothing. He grabs a newspaper and picks up his coffee. Half-way up the steps to the top bunk he opens the curtain. I am lying on his bed. All I said was "Boo". The coffee hit the ceiling and Barry went into freefall. A chair got broken, the catering crew turned up with a mop, I got some cleaning to do and then found myself before the Senior Toolpusher. It's his rig and normally he wouldn't be dealing with such trivial things but the medic had been to see him. Having nothing else to report all trip he thought he would mention this. Anyway, after I explained what had happened the tool pusher just pissed himself laughing. He was still laughing when I left his office. The medic never saw the funny side and Barry was at the three hundred marker with 'twat'. Anyway, I ended the trip with the words of Walt Whitman.

> *O Captain my Captain! Our fearful trip is done,*
> *The ship has weathered every rack, the prize we sought is won,*
> *The port is near, the bells I hear, the people all exulting,*
> *While follow eyes the steady keel, the vessel grim and daring;*

But O heart! Heart! Heart!
O the bleeding drops of red,
Where on the deck my Captain lies,
Fallen cold and dead.

Barry took the book off me and read the remainder himself. "Twat," he then muttered.

THURSDAY APRIL 19TH

After a fifteen-minute flight to the beach we were stood before Customs, going through the usual declarations. One of the drillers called Mark opened his bag and showed a single packet of piped tobacco. As he was about the close his bag the Customs guy stopped him. He then picked up the flattened packet in question and began to bounce it in his hand. "This is a little heavy isn't it?" Mark just shrugged his shoulders, "I just got it this morning from the bond." The Customs guy then produces a set of scales from under the table. Sure enough the packet it twice as heavy as it should be. Mark's bag then gets a thorough check before he is body searched. "Take off your shoes," orders the Customs guy. Mark does as he is told and as the shoes get checked he rocks back on his feet. The Customs guy notices it and asks him to take off his socks. Strapped to the bottom of each foot was another packet. Mark was taken into a side room and we quickly moved on. I just hope he hadn't stashed anymore somewhere else.

Trip Five

Wednesday May 2ND

After the usual farewells I drive down to the Gables Hotel in Blackpool. After a quiet meal and I few beers I head back to my room and take a horizontal position in front of the TV. Half an hour in and someone is attempting to punch my door in. I open it to find Big John, our welding inspector, standing there. Now I'm 6' 4" and of medium build. He is a 6' 5" pipe-smoking Aberdonian and he's built like a brick shithouse. He calls me 'the bern' an endearing term for a child. If you are a stranger then you get called 'pilgrim' until he can find a suitable tag for you. "Come on, bern," he says. "Let's have a few beers in that Star Bar." It's not a request it's a polite order.

Half a dozen beers later we are sitting at the bar and downwind of us there is a pack of animals taking the piss out of the barmaid. One loudmouth in particular is giving her a right old time. "Excuse me, pilgrim," Big John announces, "That's enough now, ok?" Now there were about eight of them and they all looked a bit handy. "Steady on, big fella," I say, "Offshore tomorrow remember?" Loudmouth doesn't give Big John a moment to think on my words. He gobs off so it's outside to the car park. They line up, Big John hands me his coat and pipe and just says, "Won't be a moment, bern." Loudmouth steps forward and Big John hit him so hard and fast I'm sure the poor kid thought he had been surrounded. As he hit the deck everyone else backed away. Back in the bar we are finishing the beer when the rest of the pack comes over. They apologise and while doing so, tell Big John he has just knocked out a local boxer that's just become a contender for some Mickey Mouse belt. "Jessies," Big John says as they depart. "This place is full of Big Jessies." I'm saying nothing.

THURSDAY MAY 3RD

It was Barry's birthday a few days ago and so his kids have bought him a brand new alarm clock. It's a football figure with the clock positioned in the centre of his body. The player's right leg swings forward to 'tick' and then swings back to 'tock'. The damn thing was deafening in the room so I put my music on whilst I thought about something to write. About one minute later I saw the alarm clock hit the opposite wall and then smash into tiny pieces. When I removed my headphones all was quiet. Barry did mutter something under his breath and I quietly left him to it.

FRIDAY MAY 4TH

The ninja arrived on board a day late because he had been bumped off the chopper the previous day because of urgent hotshot materials that were needed on board. Oil companies use this procedure all the time when they can't wait for such items to be shipped out on a boat. Most lads don't complain as they are on pay and could even get an extra night onshore at the company's expense. When I say 'most' that doesn't include ninjas who tend to take such things to heart. Anyway the ninja wasn't the only one and yes there were a shipment of papers on the chopper, so as you can imagine, Oink had a field day with it all. The first thing he did when he came into the office was to ask the ninja what it was like to be less important than the copy of a *Daily Star* newspaper. Within an hour the newspaper in question was on the ninja's desk with a modified headline that read, 'Ninjas going cheap'. We then had a copy of the chopper manifest pinned to our door with the name ninja scribbled out and replaced by a shipment of eighty rolls of shithouse paper and a *Daily Star*. It wasn't doing his blood pressure any good.

SATURDAY MAY 5TH

Oink came into the office to check on a few data sheets and as soon as he put on his Joe 90 specs the ninja couldn't resist in having a go at him. "Getting old are we, Granddad? Eyes not what they used to be? You could have at least got a pair of specs that were in fashion." Oink takes them off to counter. "I only need them for reading things up close, Ninja. I have no problems with distant objects. For example, that picture of the baby seal you have on your desk is easy to make out." The ninja frantically looks around before asking, "What baby seal, you blind git?"

"The one in the little blue dress." The ninja then homes in on the picture of his daughter. Well that was it, tables and chairs went flying and Oink just managed to escape out of the door. The ninja set off after him. Everyone is used to it now; it's like watching that Wile E Coyote and the roadrunner. Even the lads shout "beep beep" as they go tearing past.

SUNDAY MAY 6TH

Trevor and Eric came into the gym tonight but putting in a session was the last thing on their minds. They went onto the scales and that's when Trevor started to give Eric dog's abuse about the amount of weight he had been putting on. I got dragged into it somehow and Trevor made Eric tell me about his midnight feasts. One of them was the night before coming offshore when the two of them had been out on the drink and on the way home Eric bought a curry. They had a few more beers in the bar, a night cap in the room and Eric had the curry before bed. Trevor was on his case straight away and in the end Eric left as he wanted to catch the movie. Trevor laughed and then told me that he had eaten the curry that night. Apparently Eric had fallen asleep and so Trevor had the meal and before he left the room his poured some of the sauce down Eric's t-shirt and placed the empty container in his lap. The next morning Eric couldn't remember eating it and Trevor called him all the greedy gets under the sun. He then made him believe that he ate it right in front of Trevor and refused to give him any.

MONDAY MAY 7TH

Trace heating is a system used to either maintain or raise the temperature of pipes and vessels. Heating elements or tapes are run in physical contact along the lengths of pipes and are then insulated to retain the heat loss from the pipe. The heat generated protects the pipe from freezing and prevents its contents from solidifying at ambient temperatures. It's always best to do such a job when the workforce numbers start to decrease, like they are on here, as less damage can be done to the tapes. Bobby, the electrical construction engineer, has got his team on it now. I went to see him today about closing out a few of his job cards and in doing so I saw one of the best explanations of how it's actually coordinated. Now Bobby is a typical down-to-earth Geordie and the guy that interrupted us to ask about the progress of it was a big daft rough and ready company yank by the name of Randy. There was no excuse me, kiss my arse or anything he just steamrolled over me and fired his question right at Bobby. He then looked at me before rising to his chair and pointing to the layout drawings on his wall. "Right bonnie lad, ower here we've got allll the doings and ower here we've got all the shite. What we gonna de is batter all the doings in and as for the shite, well were gonna just hoy it awl outa tha winda. Bob's yer uncle and Fannie's yer aunt. Al reet?" As the yank walked away, Bobby shouted, "Don't let the door hit you on the way out and don't forget to have a shite day, won't ya." I couldn't have put in better myself.

TUESDAY MAY 8TH

I walked back over the bridge to the jack-up with Trevor. When we get to the other side we see a guy painting a pipe support. His overalls are dotted with paint and so is his face. He has the name 'Fred' penned on the pocket in big black letters. Trevor digs me in the ribs and we walk over. "Are you Fred the painter?" The guy jumps to his feet. "Yep why?" Trevor shakes his head. "You are in deep shit, wee man. According to your gaffer you will have all the supports done by lunchtime. Told all the managers in the meeting we've just had." The guy is slowly slipping into a panic. "There's no way…" Trevor holds up his hand. "Look don't shoot the messenger, I'm just giving you a heads up that's all." The guys nods, thanks him and goes crazy with the brush. We left him to it and went to lunch. On the way out we see Fred in the tea shack. He's soaked in sweat, tea in one hand and fag in the other. "Good lunch, wee man?" says Trevor. "No time for that," says Fred. "Got to get on." As we crossed the bridge, his gaffer walked by. "Have you see Fred, Trevor?" he asked.

"That lazy bastard," he replied. "He'll probably be in the tea shack. He spends most of his life in there." The gaffer set off like a train.

WEDNESDAY MAY 9TH

During the afternoon break it was all quiet and the ninja was attempting to do the cryptic crossword in the *Daily Mirror*. As he struggled away Oink came in and just laughed at him. He called the paper a comic and said its crossword was just something to keep spoon brains busy for a while. It's supposed to be a coffee break crossword and to be honest the ninja couldn't do it over a ten-course meal. Oink reckons he could do it in less than ten minutes. It had taken the ninja that long to get five clues right. The challenge was on, the Rolex became the official timepiece and Oink took over the crossword. Sure enough eight minutes later it had been completed. He held up the paper so that we could see all the boxes filled in and laughed away at the ninja. On the way out of the office he tapped him over the head with it and then threw it on the desk. It took about five seconds for the ninja erupt before darting after him. Upon close inspection the crossword had been completed but Oink had filled it in with the first words that had come into his head. He even managed to get such favourites as 'watch', 'shite', 'crap', 'bollocks', and 'ninja' in there. He managed all that in just eight minutes, the man is a genius. The ninja doesn't seem to think so.

THURSDAY MAY 10TH

The door to our office faces south and as we are at quite a height when the wind gets up, then it becomes quite a task to get either in or out. Our office is an A60 rated unit, the 'A' being the maximum cellulosic fire temperature and the 60 defines the time during which the unexposed face must not exceed a temperature of 188°C. So as you can imagine the office door is quite heavy and in high winds you always get help to get in and out. Today we had the wind coming right at the door and did our best to help all visitors in. That stopped at tea break and that's when Ron, one of the piping engineers, tried to get in. First it was door open, door slammed shut. That was repeated a few times before it was door open and arm in. That was followed by trapped arm, squeal like a baby, door slammed shut. Then we had door open, arm and head in, a cry for help, door slammed shut. We then heard a torrent of abuse, door yanked open, arm in, head in, body in, legs in, door slammed shut. As he caught his breath and we continue drinking tea he eventually pulled a drawing out of his pocket. He went to walk over to the corner of the office and stopped as he noticed it was just an empty area. He then turned to me and asked, "Where is the photocopier?"

"They moved it next door last thing yesterday," I replied. When he turned to face the door he had just fought through we all fell about laughing. We continued to do so as he went through the same painful routine again. I have never heard so many curse words in such a small space of time.

FRIDAY MAY 11TH

At the morning meeting today we were told that if all goes to plan our next trip will be the last one on this platform. We are getting to the stage now where it's all down to operations. They are gradually manning up so we have to do the standard phase down man. We can see the platform some of us are going to as it's only a few miles away from where we are now. Some of the lads won't be needed as their slots have already been filled on the other installation. When all is said and done, it's the nature of the game.

This is a good platform and it has been engineered and built by some fine people and I will miss them. The next few trips will see a lot of handshakes, reminders to keep in touch and most important of all, the exchange of CVs, just in case a nice number comes up and they need someone.

SATURDAY MAY 12TH

When you look at the divers offshore you realise just how easy the end of a shift is to you. You just walk away and do what you need to do to wind down and relax. They have to guard against decompression sickness (DCS) where nitrogen bubbles in the blood have not had time to be released safely. It can bring on joint pain, paralysis, fatigue, skin rash, vertigo, amnesia and unconsciousness. It can be treated in a decompression chamber, which is like ending your shift in a little prison cell. Give me the gym or a movie any day.

SUNDAY MAY 13TH

Due to hotshot material requirements we had a few flights in today and that meant newspapers. I managed to get my hands on one and amongst all the scandal, wars and adverts for cheap crap I found a heart-warming story. A little girl needed a lifesaving operation and the best blood match was her little brother. In the presence of his parents he was asked by the doctor to donate a few pints. He hesitated for a moment before finally saying yes. The transfusion and operation went by without a hitch and the young girl was going to make a full recovery. The doctor gave the parents the good news and then they all went to see the little brother to let him know. As soon as they entered the room he asked them how his sister was and smiled when he learnt that she was going to be ok. His mood then darkened a little as he looked at the plaster on his arm. He then turned to the doctor and with a tremble in his voice asked, "How quickly will I start to die?" It may be cheap words to some I know but every now and then a story like that does give you a lift.

MONDAY MAY 14TH

Being away from home affects people in different ways, most people just switch off and get on with the job. Some turn into right miserable bastards right up until the last day and then all of a sudden they morph into Mr Happy. Some count their life away whilst others lose track of all time and just let one day turn into the next. Today, in the tea shack, I met Dennis, one of the ops technicians, and he was smoking like a chimney. He doesn't smoke at home. He told me that he hates being away from his family so much that he uses the fags to calm his nerves. Apparently he gets spells of mild depression and so the fags manage to get him through them. He's got debts and needs the money so at the moment he's in a vicious circle. I only hope he manages to get out of it sometime soon.

TUESDAY MAY 15TH

Shell Oil went through a phase whereby all their platforms were named after birds. They had the likes of Auk, Cormorant, Eider, Gannet, Kittiwake, Osprey, Shearwater, and Tern. Today we got notification of their 'Parrot' project. It was a professionally done bulletin with a parrot perched on top of the Shell logo. There were details on the field development in the North Sea and there was a contact address and phone number for their headquarters in The Hague, Netherlands. The ninja was on it in a flash. He then had a ten-minute phone conversation with a bemused cloggy about getting an application for the Parrot. Just as the ninja was about to put the phone down he looked up to see Oink standing on one leg, patch over one eye and a battery operated parrot on his shoulder. It was one of those toys that just repeated whatever you said to it and flapped its wings whilst doing so. When Oink switched it on it squawked, "Hey ninja, wanna job on my platform?" He must have recorded it then switched it off before he came in. Anyway I dread to think what was going through the mind of that cloggy on the end of the phone as he listened to the confrontation that followed.

WEDNESDAY MAY 16TH

A storeman is usually someone that holds materials until you need them and readily hands them out when required. Our storeman is a staffy called Russell and he thinks a storeman is just someone that stores things. Trying to get anything out of him is like trying to get blood out of a stone. If you take three items out and only use two then he wants the third one back regardless if you need it the next day or not.

A lamp is something that produces light, it's not a bulb it's a lamp. If you mention the word 'bulb' in front of a spark he will simply say, "You get bulbs in a garden centre, in this game we use lamps."

This morning one of Trevor's boys took out four lamps and duly returned one. Well when I say one, he returned one box. The lamp had been removed and replaced by a turd. As you can imagine the day got warmer and the store soon became unbearable. Apparently Russell had turned all shades of green by the time a few of the lads donned BA sets to go in and find out what the problem was. Nothing was found and the store was aired so that Russell could go back to storing things. If he had looked close enough he would have noticed that one of his bulbs had gone.

THURSDAY MAY 17TH

A local airline has put on flights to Teesside and as they are only thirty quid for a thirty-minute flight a few of us gave it a go. Firstly, it wasn't a plane it was a flying skip. Secondly, it wasn't spacious as there were only six seats on the plane. Lastly, cabin service consisted of a girl that sat besides the pilot, handing us a flask and a stack of cups. Ten minutes into the flight the alcohol drinks trolley arrived. Well, what I mean is we were handed a shopping bag full of miniatures. I passed but Derek, one of our planners, just about poured the bag over his head. By the time we got to Teesside airport he was all over the place. Some guys just seem to forget that after two weeks off the drink you get pissed a lot quicker than you imagine. When we arrived at Teesside I was straight through and the wife was there to meet me. I then saw a girl with two boys waiting in anticipation for the return of a husband and father. Well he appeared with an almighty bang. I turned just in time to see the arrivals door swing open. Derek had a bag in each hand and so he had to use his head to open the door. Once through he just kept going, head down, into the main body of the airport. His wife then ran across the floor and caught him like a baseball. She then spun him around and aimed him at the exit. As they moved off the two boys just stood open-mouthed. Welcome home.

TRIP SIX

WEDNESDAY MAY 30TH

I t was Groundhog Day again. I'm in my room at the Gables Hotel and Big John is trying to punch a hole in my door. There is no way I'm going this time, this time I'm staying put. Anyway, a few beers later after doing a circuit we end up in the Blue Lion pub. "Do you want a ticket, lad?" asks this weird-looking misfit that resembled Gollum from *The Lord of the Rings* novel. "How much are they?" I ask.

"Just a pound each," he sneers.

"We'll take two, pilgrim," began Big John. "Pay the man, bern," he adds. I give Gollum two quid and he goes straight to the bar with it and buys a drink. As I look on in dismay Big John goes over to the bar and lifts him clean off the floor with one hand. "Explain yourself, pilgrim," he asks.

"It's all real, man," replies the trembling hobbit. "When we draw it if you win I will go and steal what you want tomorrow." If ever there was a raffle I didn't want to win that was it and luckily we didn't.

THURSDAY MAY 31ST

After reading my handover notes and noting that this is going to be my last trip on here I went to see Trevor and the boys and dropped a few newspapers on his desk. The crack is all about which famous people they have met and chatted to. When I'm asked I rattle off a load of punk rock stars as I saw at The Middlesbrough Rock Garden. I then mention Paul Weller in Carnaby Street, Richard Dunn whilst offshore and then I'm stopped. They wanted me to tell them the boxer story.

After giving up boxing Richard went back to working offshore as a scaffolder. He used to run two shows in the cinema with all the proceeds going to charity. At the first you watched his fight with Ali and at the second you watched him on the TV show *This is Your Life*. Both included question and answers sessions. At the first one I asked him what was going through his mind after the bell rang to start the fifth round against Ali. The reason I asked is that Ali was telling the world beforehand that he was going to put Dunn down in five. Richard answered, "When we came out for the first he said to me, 'Ok Richard, let's dance but remember you're going down in five.'" He then continued rounds two, three and four with the same line. "When it came to round five I thought, right mate you're getting the lot here. The bell rang, I walked towards him and the next thing I remember I'm lying on the canvas with a second flicking a towel over me asking, 'Richard, Richard, are you alright?'" I also remembered him telling us all that Ali got one million dollars for the fight and he got fifty thousand pounds. He ended up with thirty thousand of it. The lads then ask Trevor to tell me about the famous celeb he once met offshore. He was getting quite a ribbing over it and was saying nothing. Anyway, he was saved by the bell as the alarm went off and we all had to muster. It was another false alarm.

FRIDAY JUNE 1ST

I spent a good hour with old Walter from the welding department today and he confided in me that he wasn't going to the new platform with us as he has decided to call it a day and retire. He spoke with pride about what he had achieved and noted that he could have done more if he had stuck in at school. He made no excuses and just blamed himself for wasting too much time, time he had spent the rest of his life trying to catch up with. Before I left him I tugged on his overalls and said, "Hey mate, we all wear these big boys' romper suits of success."

"Bollocks," he joked. "This trip I have achieved jack shit so for now they are the robes of failure."

SATURDAY JUNE 2ND

And that's not all. According to Trevor, that was the only line actor Colin Welland had to say. At the time he was doing a lot of 'Health and Safety' videos for British Gas so the director thought it best to do a few offshore. He set up a scene near the lifeboat area and Trevor and the boys were there just in case he needed anything. Anyway "Take one" and Colin walks in front of the lifeboat and delivers his line to perfection. Something not right, thinks the director. He has a think for a while and looks at the boys 'eureka'. He asks if the lads can act as extras. Nothing too difficult, just pretend to be working in the background. Trevor sends one Geordie lad to a nearby telephone stand and another to the muster rack.

"Take two," shouts the director. "And that's—"

"Hang on a bit, bonnie lad," interrupts the first Geordie "Where's my pormit?"

"Pormit?" screams the director. Trevor steps into the shot.

"Permit bigun, permit. He shouldn't be here without a work permit."

"What the hell—" begins the director before Trevor cuts across him.

"Cool your jets bigun, I have one here." Trevor then goes and hangs a permit on the stand.

"Take three. And that's not—" "Woah, bonnie lad," says the second Geordie. "I'm instruments not mechanical, this is a job for a mechy."

"Who the hell will know?" screams the director.

"Billy and Tommy from my agency would. Not to mention all the lads down the club. And then there's—"

"Right, right, right, get me a mechy!" screams the director. Trevor looked at his watch.

"No chance bigun, they are all watching the match."

"Right, right, fuck off the lot of you!" screamed the director. According to Trevor, Colin Welland was laughing his head off.

SUNDAY JUNE 3RD

There were two angels walking down the road. One was old and wise and the other was young and what usually goes with it. Anyway, as they approached a nearby settlement it began to rain so they approached a house in search of shelter. They had to plead with the nasty young couple that answered the door before being allowed access. Eventually they were given short words and a cold damp cellar for their troubles. It was an evening the young angel would never forget. He had never been so cold in his life. The room was dark, the floor was wet and the walls were full of holes. Although the wind easily found his bones, he did manage to steal a few hours of sleep. When he awoke he was not surprised to see the old angel moving about but he was surprised to see that he had fixed the walls. He said nothing. Without an offer of food or a goodbye they were on their way once more. Once again they reached a settlement just as a storm was brewing. They found a house and a kindly old couple that welcomed them in with open arms. They gave them hot food and one of their bedrooms to stay in. The young angel slept soundly. When he awoke he found the old angel in the kitchen with the old couple. They were in tears. Looking out of the window he then saw that their milk-providing cow lay dead in the field. After he had chance to console the old couple he and his mentor moved on. A few miles down the road he stopped and confronted his older companion. He wanted to know why he had helped the nasty couple with their wall but then allowed the cow of the nice couple to die. "As you slept in the cellar," he began. "I looked at the walls and noticed that treasure had been hidden beyond them. Not wanting the nasty couple to have it I sealed the walls. As for last night, as you slept the angel of death appeared. He wanted to take the old woman. I pleaded with him but he had come for a soul and could not leave without one. We then agreed on the cow."

The reason I wrote that is that I was reminded not to judge a book by its cover. In a meeting with the contractor some of our managers were intent on giving their general foreman a hard time on progress. His name was Jimmy, no-one noticed him enter the room or take his seat, well I say no-one, I did. He had an air of confidence about him and when he was eventually put on the spot in the meeting it was a joy to watch. He used words that had some reaching for dictionaries. He fended off every question that was thrown at him and then went on the attack. I sat and watched as some of our team began to slide down their seats. By the time he had finished he had secured more money for his company. I later learnt that everyone calls him 'The Articulate Bear'. This definitely is a space worth watching.

MONDAY JUNE 4TH

I rang home for a chat with the wife about the daughter's up and coming graduation day when she gives me a name and number to ring. It's an agency that wants me to go to London for an interview for a job in Kazakhstan. The rota is six and two and the money is good so I say yes. The Karachaganak Project was mentioned as well as a little town by the name of Aksai. I search the web and look over the few details that are available on the contract. I then have a look at the country itself.

Kazakhstan is in Central Asia, south of Russia and North West of China. By area it's the ninth largest landmass in the world and the largest landlocked country. The place is four times the size of Texas, five times the size of France and is only habited by fifteen million people. It became independent from Russia in 1991. Its President is Nursultan Nazarbayev, its capital is Astana and its currency, which is not recognised anywhere else in the world, is called the Tenge. This place has three time zones and it's where the first manned space flight took off from in 1961. When you look at the map of it you see deserts, steppes, savannahs, taiga, tundra, enormous forests, massive lakes and rivers that run for miles and miles. It's a hidden gem and right now I want to be part of it.

TUESDAY JUNE 5TH

Well it was a strange shift. The ninja was banging on about his Rolex again when Oink strolled in. "For fuck's sake, sparrow legs, stop going on about that trick watch will you." The ninja gets upset so Oink plays it out. He shows him his ten petrol voucher quartz watch and declares, "This is waterproof."

"So is this," replies ninja.

"This is heat resistant,"

"So is this," repeats ninja.

"This is waterproof and heat resistant at the same time," announces Oink. The ninja hesitates and then gets out his guarantee. There is nothing about combined resistance. "It's a trick watch," laughs Oink. "You spent a fortune on a trick watch." The ninja almost exploded and then Oink asks him to put it to the test. He agrees without hesitation. This is when it all got a little strange. Oink went over to the kettle, switched it on and dropped his watch inside. "Right then, come on," he says. The ninja hesitated but not wanting to lose face did exactly the same. Oink put the lid on and the whole office watched in silence as it boiled. Straight away Oink poured the water into nearby cups and turned the kettle upside down. His watch came out as a black mangled piece of goo and the ninja's looked to be ok. When he eventually managed to check it he found that it had stopped and he couldn't get it to work again. Oink scooped what was left of his into the bin and pulled another identical one out of his pocket. As he strapped it on he said to ninja, "Told you it was a trick watch." That was it; the ninja went berserk and chased him out of the office.

WEDNESDAY JUNE 6TH

Young Simon, one of the welders, is getting married when he goes on leave. The only reason I know this is that on the end of shift walkabout I saw him on the cellar neck. He was near the bridge, he was tied to a beam, he was bollock naked and covered in all kinds of crap. Now when you see something like this the best thing to do is keep out of it. So as he shivered away the only thing one of our group was allowed to do was to straighten the sign around his neck that said 'Dickhead'.

My offshore survival is due for renewal so I have organised it for the back end of my leave. As I am still within the four years of cover and I will only have to do a three-day refresher and not the full five-day course.

THURSDAY JUNE 7TH

Every week we are expected to put safety observations in to ensure we are working towards an accident-free project. Basically, you are allocated a buddy and the both of you then have to go on a safety walk to check the on-going working practices. If someone is doing it right you commend them and if they are breaking the rules then you stop them and have a chat about it. Cards get filled in and no names are mentioned. According to the clever people it's all about spotting trends so that awareness campaigns can be introduced to either remind or re-educate people on what their responsibilities are. I went with Billy today and apart from people not using three points of contact on the stairwells nothing much was out of order. That changed as soon as we reached the drilling module. Billy and I soon found ourselves standing in streams of mud. One of the hoses had split and now the deck was getting covered. We rang Les, the engineer in charge, and the next thing you know there were people swarming all over the place. When the OIM saw it he went to about thirty thousand feet before coming back down. The clean up exercise is expected to last for some time. Billy filled the observation card in and got a baseball cap, a cup and a key ring. I got a pair of muddy boots.

FRIDAY JUNE 8TH

I think it's safe to say that Rolf and Hank don't get on. Rolf is electrical commissioning and Hank is electrical construction. Rolf is German and Hank is American. Rolf is the one that needs a temporary cable installing and Hank is the one messing it up. It was a simple job that should have taken no more than a few hours and we are now at day three and it's still not finished. Add to the fact that Hank is going home today and it's simple to see why Rolf is having a fit. It got out of hand so much that the OIM had to step in and advise Hank that he wouldn't be on the chopper until the job was done. How do I know all this? Well, Hank dashed into my office today in his survival suit to throw the completed job card at me. The chopper was almost on deck so I was asked to inform the irate German. Anyway, after Hank had left Rolf came to see me to see if everything was in order. I told him that everything was fine apart from the as-built sketch.

As you can imagine in our game we deal with all types of drawings raging from Piping & Instrument Diagrams (PIDs), Electrical Termination Diagrams (ETDs), Single Line Diagrams (SLDs), Instrument Loop Drawings (LOPs) to various vendor supplied drawings. With this being a temporary cable there was no drawing in existence to red line with the temporary cable so Hank was asked to produce an as-built sketch.

Rolf's hands were trembling. In it was a single sheet of A4 paper. On the left-hand side of it was an orange-crayoned box with four lines under it with the word 'jack-up' scribbled on it. On the right was a brown box with eight lines under it and the words 'Oil rig' written on it. The black rectangle that connected them both carried the word 'bridge'. The four blue wavy lines beneath it all was the sea, the bright yellow circle in the top right hand corner was the sun and two sea gulls could be seen flying across it all. The red line that ran from the jack-up, across the bridge and onto the oil rig was the temporary cable. The source of the cable was marked with the words 'It starts here' and the other end of it had the words 'It ends here'. It has to be said that the little man that had been drawn standing near the cable did resemble Rolf a little.

When the chopper lifted off the deck Hank could have been forgiven for thinking that the figure jumping up and down beneath him was just wishing him farewell.

SATURDAY JUNE 9TH

Apparently Gideons' place more than 45,000,000 bibles annually in prisons, hospitals, military bases and hotels. Well someone had the idea that we need them out here as they have appeared in our rooms. At the safety meeting today Phil the safety rep tabled his objection to it all on the grounds that he is a born again atheist. When he was informed that his would be removed he asked the OIM if such literature was in his library. The reason he asked was that all OIMs have a library that contain all manner of documents ranging from rules, regulations and laws right down to the Cullen Report on the Piper Alpha disaster. It is an open library and to our surprise the OIM he admitted that he had a copy of the King James Bible in there. That's when it descended into a farce. "What about the Koran?" asks Phil.

"Er No," replied the OIM.

"What about the Torah?"

"No."

"The Mahabharata."

"No." Phil now wants to know about what prejudices the OIM has against Islam, Judaism and Hinduism. After confirming that he doesn't have any he assures Phil that the Bible will be removed so as not to offend anyone. Later in the day all the Gideons' were removed. I am sure some hotel in Blackpool will be underwhelmed sometime soon.

SUNDAY JUNE 10TH

Two men were to appear before a judge for stealing poultry. The innocent man was going to leave it to the system but the guilty man had no such plans. He went to see a well-respected lawyer and asked him to take up his case. The lawyer listened to the evidence, observed that it was going to be difficult but took it on anyway. When the guilty man suggested that he could send the judge a few chickens with a note the lawyer was adamant that he shouldn't for he would surely lose the case. The day of the trial arrived, the case was heard and the innocent man was found guilty and the guilty man was found innocent. Afterwards the lawyer was happy that he didn't have to resort to any tricks. In turning to his client he said, "You see, I told you that if you had sent the judge those chickens you would have lost."

"I sent them anyway," replied his client. "But I put the other man's name on the note."

It's all about being crafty I suppose and boy are our planners good at it. At the beginning of the day we were well below the progress curve but by the end of it we were above it. I tried to work it out but failed drastically. Then old

Tom showed me what he had done. When he was onshore he got a few of the engineers to create a few duplicate none too cleverly descripted job cards that were approved using fictitious signatures for work that had been covered elsewhere. These were well-hidden in the plan and were Tom's 'get out of jail' cards. Anyway a few timesheets were booked to them and before you knew it we were looking good again.

MONDAY JUNE 11TH

Eve, the black widow, has arrived on-board today. She is from the personnel department and has come to give the kiss of death to the people that won't be needed on the next platform. Yes, this platform is full of grown men who are used to getting paid off at a moment's notice but what they are doing here is a disgrace. People's names are getting announced over the tannoy system followed by a polite request to go and see her. It not only lacks respect it does nothing for dignity. To show this the lads have got together and as soon as a name is called a black spot gets painted on the centre of their hats. Some even have legs protruding from them. This is not a day to be proud of this industry.

TUESDAY JUNE 12TH

I spent the full day helping the materials group with the transfer of surplus materials. Just as we thought we had everything ready for the boat I hear my name on the radio. It's Dave, the one-armed bandit, who works for operations. He lost part of his right arm in a car accident and it has been replaced by a hook. It's a brace affair that runs around his shoulders so to open it he has to push his left arm forward. You just have to remember not to stand too close when he does. Anyway I find him on the cellar deck grinning like a Cheshire cat. "I thought you so-called professionals had back loaded everything?" he bawled.

"We have," I said. He then points to a rack beside one of the containers. "Then what are those pipe spools doing there?" he asked.

"Acting like scaffold poles," I replied. I couldn't believe it. The scaffolders had dismantled their gear and had housed it correctly in a rack they had been using throughout the project; a project old hooky had been on for quite a while, with a rack he had walked past several times. He went bright red and asked me to say nothing. I did mention it to Trevor and he accidentally announced it over the platform tannoy system.

WEDNESDAY JUNE 13TH

This morning I could have had boiled Rolex Oyster for breakfast. Well that's what was on the menu board in the galley. You couldn't miss it as it was surrounded in pictures of watches. The ninja never noticed it at first. He got the message when people began to sit at our table with watches on their plates. You could see that he wanted to explode but he held it all in. He lasted until he got to our office. All Oink did was walk in and hold up the kettle and ask him if he wanted a drink. The outside of the kettle was full of watch pictures. Well the ninja just erupted and once again the chase began. It lasted for about thirty minutes before the ninja managed to get back to his desk. As soon as he sat down the tannoy binged and a well-known voice said, "The time after the beeps will be 08.00 exactly. This does not apply to trick watched ninjas, beep, beep, oooooiiiiiiinnnnnnnnnnnk." The ninja just took his head in his hands and slowly placed it on the desk.

I spent most of the day saying goodbye to people. That poet was right; there is no good in a goodbye.

THURSDAY JUNE 14TH

As I write this I am about to get on a chopper flight that should have happened five hours ago. A mist descended on the bay earlier in the day and the flights were grounded. The one that did leave the deck here for the beach had to return because of low visibility. It's unusual for them to do that as land is easier to get to than a platform but apparently the mist is hugging a vast stretch of the coastline. The pilots did explain the details to those that were listening and the term 'legal' was being used quite a lot. I wasn't there but apparently one of the lads that was on the flight and not best pleased about it all simply screamed, "For fuck's sake man, I could see a Labrador having a shit on the beach. How clear does it have to be?" Anyway the chopper is on deck and the clock is ticking.

TRIP SEVEN

SUNDAY JUNE 24TH

Well the interview for Kazakhstan went well, and as they think it over, it's offshore survival course time, so I got the train out of Darlington and settled down for a quiet five hours to Aberdeen.

I had my papers, my music and the usual snacks. The journey remained uneventful until I reached Edinburgh. A couple of lads that were going offshore the following morning arrived and sat opposite me while a suited city gent took a seat on the other side of the train. As the three of us struck up a conversation we noticed the city gent opening his briefcase. Out of it came an empty sandwich wrapper, an empty packet of crisps and an empty can. City gent then proceeds to fake a sleep. We look on in bewilderment and then when we hear an inspector close in and announce, "Tickets from Edinburgh, all tickets from Edinburgh please." The lads opposite duly oblige and city gent gets away with it. That's how it remained all the way to Aberdeen until one of the lads opposite intervened. As the inspector did his final pass he stopped him and then shouted, "Hey mate, here is the inspector you were asking about. He can sort a ticket for you." Well if looks could kill. He got hit for the full fare and was let off with a warning.

MONDAY JUNE 25TH

Day one at the Robert Gordon Institute of Technology (RGIT) and after initial registration they tell us what's in store for us over the next few days. We then watch a few videos and do the usual questions and answers on all aspects of personal safety. Lunch is followed by a bit of fire fighting. Not as extensive as the full course at Montrose so it's a relaxed atmosphere. Once we have extinguished a few fires and crawled in and around smoke-filled rooms it's back in the classroom. For homework we are asked to listen to *Staying Alive* by the Bee Gees. As luck has it it's on one of my tapes.

TUESDAY JUNE 26TH

Day two and we spend the morning in the pool. Over your cossie you wear a thin pair of overalls and on your head is a plastic hat, it's blue if you can swim and red if you can't. In addition to that you get to wear a lifejacket. You then go over the exercise you first did on the full course. You have to jump from a height into the pool and then tread water for a while. You then have to climb up a rope ladder. Next it's swimming to an overturned liferaft so that you can climb on and turn it upright. It all ends with the whole class swimming to the raft, helping each other in and then locking it down. As you do this one of the instructors spray cold water over you from hoses just to give it a bit of reality.

The afternoon of videos and discussion classes was mixed in with first aid training. As part of it you go over putting people in the recovery position and administrating cardiopulmonary resuscitation or CPR. Using the head and torso section of a dummy you run through the required procedure as you would on any human. You check for consciousness and a pulse and a clear airway. You put the person on a firm flat surface. Hands interlocked straight down from your shoulder you compress the chest area thirty times. You then pinch the person's nose, tilt their head back and administer mouth-to-mouth twice and check on the rise and fall of the chest. Now this is done to a ratio and it keeps changing but if you get it slightly wrong but the patient lives I'm sure they will forgive you. As for the tempo of it all, think Bee Gees and *Staying Alive*. As we did ours, the instructors had the song as background noise and believe me it worked.

WEDNESDAY JUNE 27TH

Last day of the refresher course and the only thing we have to do is escape from a ditched helicopter. Basically, they have cylinder with cut out doors and windows suspended on a winch over the pool. In it are a few chairs with safety belts. In teams of four you get in and go through some stages. It's lowered into the water waist height and you unbuckle your belt and step out into the water. It's lowered into the water just above head height and you unbuckle your belt and swim out of your allocated window. It lowered into the water and rotates through one hundred and eighty degrees. You remain suspended upside down until the bubbles settle and then you swim out of the nearest window. Finally, you do the one eighty again but this time they have put windows in so you have to punch them out before escaping. It's bad enough having to do this if you can swim so my heart always goes out to the red-hatted non-swimmers. There were two of them in my team. One was called Mick and he almost swallowed half the pool during the last exercise but he scraped through. Keith, on the other hand, was as cool as ice with it all. When I asked him about it he told me that not only could he swim he had his scuba diving master's certificate. Mick's face was a picture. Job done it's a train journey to Blackpool and a quiet night in before the new adventure.

THURSDAY JUNE 28TH

Well it's the first day on a new platform and as the boys have already got the systems for habitation up we will be working towards the drilling targets. Firstly, it's new inductions followed by a bit of desk arranging and box opening. We all thought the Irish jack-up manager was ok until he burst into our office and slammed the door. As we all looked up he shouted, "Right, there is a fire in the corridor so what are you going to do?"

"You what?" asks our process engineer, Stuart.

"I said there is a fire so what are you going to do?"

"Solids, liquids or gasses?" asks Stuart.

"You what?" bawls the manager.

"The fire," began Stuart. "Is it solid, liquids or gases?"

"Well if you're not going to take it seriously you can all burn." The manager then muttered something under his breath and stormed out. We never saw him again. Maybe there was a fire somewhere; I couldn't tell you what type though.

After a few weird hours trying settle in I came to the conclusion that I'm just not sure about this one. Part of me just hopes that the Kazakh gig comes through. Maybe it's just me but something is telling me that it's time for a change.

FRIDAY JUNE 29TH

On my desk was a note from the night shift general foreman. It read; *'Pedestal crane, diesel hydraulic system buggered, have fun. Ronnie.'* Job cards were hastily being written and the vendor was on his way out. We had to get the dossier ready and so I got after it. Five minutes later two big paws landed on my desk. I looked up to see the word 'love' across the fingers of one and 'hate' on the other. I looked up further and then realised they belonged to our new construction manager called Jim. Now this was a guy that used to be a crane driver and so I knew what was coming next. Five minutes later I felt like I was drowning in diesel. What struck me most was the way he was incorrectly using words. It was as if he was trying to sound eloquent but he was failing badly. "That vendor will be here for five, six, seven days. It could even stretch to a week." That was followed by, "I knew before anyone else because I got it up the back passage." When he left I started a list and put it on the shared drive and let everyone know where it was.

SATURDAY JUNE 30TH

The offshore industry used to be littered with bullies. They used to be the thick dinosaurs that companies used to employ as they honestly believed they got the best out of people and achieved targets quicker. All they ever did was change the mood of hook-up projects. I can almost hear their voices now. "I'll run you off here if it's the last thing I do. You will never work for this company again. I don't know why you are here, we don't need you." Sad to say one of those dinosaurs is still roaming this installation. He never introduced himself but later I found out that his name was Geoff, a construction general foreman. "What are you going to be doing here other than putting your name on a timesheet?" was the first thing he said to me.

"My, you really are little, aren't you?" was my reply.

"It must be awful when you don't accomplish anything each day," he countered.

"It must be awful being the last one to know its raining and the first one to know we're having a flood," I said, looking down at his small frame. He meant nothing to me as I didn't report to him and I was just letting him know that I was aware of his reputation and it was wasted on me. It felt good watching him storm out of the office and slam the door.

SUNDAY JULY 1ST

I met Harry, the frustrated magician, today. During most of the day he is a Non-Destructive Test (NDT) operator. When welds need to be checked to see if there are any failure points within them like slag, lack of fusion, porosity or cracks then we use NDT. Dependant on what type of weld it is it can be checked by radiography (RAD), ultrasonic inspection (UT) or magnetic particle inspection (MPI). The latter involves coating the weld in inks and running a magnetic yoke across them. If there is a defect then the magnetic flux will leak and is visible to the eye. This method is used for surface and subsurface checks and Harry has been doing it for years. He has also been doing card tricks for the same amount of time and every newcomer to the platform has to endure one or two. Pretty soon you find out he's quite good and has never forgotten the time he sent a trick to the TV magician David Nixon and was sent one pound for it. Anyway, I am about to walk away when Harry shuffles the deck for his big finale. He hands me the card off the top and then looks across the platform. "Hey Rab," he shouts to one of the lads, "Name a card, any card you like." Rab tells him where to get off but in the end calls out, "The five of clubs," and walks away. Sure enough I am holding the five of clubs.

MONDAY JULY 2ND

The message on my desk just said 'ring home' and I did so in a flash. I have got the job in Kazakhstan and the agent wants to know when I can I start. If I finish the trip here I can have two weeks off and get there on July 26th. The letter of invitation is on its way to the Kazakh embassy and I went to see the Offshore Installation Manager (OIM) to hand in my notice. He could see that my mind was already made up and knew that any attempts to talk me out of it would fall on deaf ears. He then reminisced about his days running around the planet in pursuit of the big money. He wished he was still young enough to do it and then wished me well with the decision I had taken.

TUESDAY JULY 3RD

Apparently little man Geoff likes wet fish; well that's when they haven't been nailed to the back of his desk. They were on the menu in the galley on Sunday so when he found them today that made them about three days old. Some say that he did mention the smell on Monday and since then it had increasingly got worse. He only got the catering manager involved when it had become unbearable. As you can imagine he wasn't best pleased when he was shown the cause of the stench he had been working through. Eye witnesses did mention something about a little purple-faced midget going off like a fifty bob rocket around the office. The culprit hasn't owned up yet but when he does there are plenty of people ready to shake his hand.

WEDNESDAY JULY 4TH

They say that in any given 24-hour period your heart beats 103, 681 times. Your blood travels 168,000,000 miles. You breathe 23,020 times. You inhale 437 cubic feet of air. You speak 25,000 words and you exercise 7,000,000 brain cells. Well today I met someone that makes the last two set of figures look like a joke. The management have sent out one of Geoff's old mates. He is some senile old cider-drinking foreman called Tony out to help with progress in the field and he is something to behold. His hourly word count has to be around the 20,000 mark and there don't seem to be many gaps between them. The ones you can decipher sound like they have been made up. It's not that I don't like the guy I just wouldn't want to play him at Scrabble. As for the brain cells bit the guy has a habit of staring at people and then asking, "Well?" When he gets the surprised answer of, "Well what?" he then asks the question he thinks he asked you before saying, "Well." It makes for one hell of a confusing conversation with him. My head hurts just thinking about it. For now he's on my 'clown' list and I can't see him getting off it anytime soon.

THURSDAY JULY 5TH

I bumped into Simon, the newly-married welder today. Apparently the service went off well and the honeymoon in Italy was fantastic He never said much about his stag night and I, like everyone else on the platform, was under orders not to ask about the condom. Apparently when the lads got him pissed out of his head and carried him home they got a condom and used a pencil to thread it into his arse. Ever since then people have been waiting for him to say something about it but as of yet no joy. I can't imagine what went through his mind the next morning when he found it there.

FRIDAY JULY 6TH

It's the offshore workers' remembrance day. On this day back in 1988 Occidental's Piper Alpha platform exploded killing 167 men, there were 61 survivors. We gathered on deck, had a moment of silence and then a wreath was cast into the water. The safety department put on the video of the disaster for those that needed reminding of what can go wrong. As I sat and watched it a poem written about it by one of the lads came to mind.

At 12.00pm during a routine maintenance procedure a safety valve was removed from condensate pump 'A' and the open pipe was covered by a hand-tightened blind flange. At 6.00pm the day shift ended and the duty engineer filled out his permit to say that the pump in question was not to be used. The permit was placed in the control centre. The problem was that in a different location there was another permit to work on the same pump. Although this permit had not been started it was going to get used with disastrous results. At 9.45pm problems with the methanol system hydrates had begun to form in the gas compression pipework causing a blockage in condensate pump 'B'. This pump stopped and could not be restarted and now the platform power supplies were about to fail. The manager was handed the unused permit for pump 'A' and it was signed. No-one on shift was aware that a valve was missing. At 9.55pm condensate pump 'A' was switched on.

The day shift is sleeping.
The hour is nine.
There's a valve that it missing.
On a high pressure line.
The stillness is broken.
What a terrible howl.
Demented and rabid.
Like wolves on the prowl.

The gas leaked, ignited and then blew through the firewalls. As the alarms went off, flying panels ruptured the condensate pipework and a fire broke out. At 10.04pm the control room was abandoned.

The gas is escaping.
Now fire teams await.
There's call for a muster.

But I fear it's too late.
An inferno is raging.
God I'm standing alone.
The steel it is melting.
Like the flesh from our bones.

Due to the raging fire and billowing smoke access to the lifeboats became impossible. Two men donned protective gear and attempted to reach the fire fighting system, they were lost forever. And while all this was happening the fire continued to be force fed from the Claymore and Tartan platforms. Its managers couldn't get Occidental's permission to stop production. Such decisions are down to cost but today it was going to be human not monetary.

Oh the fire is spreading.
And panic is rife.
A scaffolder cries out.
Then jumps for his life.
There's men going crazy.
And screaming in pain.
The sound of the dying.
It drives me insane.

At 10.20pm the gas line from the Tartan platform melted. The released gas ignited. Ten minutes later a large semi-submersible fire fighting vessel called *Tharos* drew up alongside the platform. It was already too late. At 10.50pm a gas line on a riser platform ruptured and drove the *Tharos* off station. The accommodation block erupted in flames and those still alive began to leap into the water from all deck levels including the helideck which stood some fifty metres above the sea. At 11.20pm the gas pipeline to the Claymore platform burst.

Up on the derrick.
A roughneck in vain.
Screams for his mother.
To come ease his pain.
Another explosion.

72

God that makes it three.
The quarters we lived in.
Now slide to the sea.

At 12.45am Module 'A' was all that remained of the Piper Alpha platform. There were 226 on the platform at the time of the disaster. One hundred and sixty-five perished along with a further two helpers from a nearby standby vessel called *Sandhaven*.

So remember the Piper.
You who are to blame.
When you're sent to the devil.
To burn in his flame.
To the lads of the Piper.
You've not died in vain.
We'll remember you always.
And inherit your pain.

The Cullen inquiry found Occidental guilty on various safety measures but no criminal charges were ever brought against them. A wreck buoy now marks the spot where it all happened. There is a sculpture to the lost in the Rose Garden of Hazlehead Park in Aberdeen. The Piper Alpha Families and Survivors Association was formed to campaign for a safer industry; they are winning.

SATURDAY JULY 7TH

If there is one place you never expect to see a thief then it's offshore. After all we are well-paid and we are in a close-knit environment where you are all supposed to look after each other. That has been soured today as 'There is a thief about' posters have gone on the notice boards. One of the lads has had his locker door wedged open and a few hundred pounds in cash has been stolen. You can feel the atmosphere around the place now. There was no need to do what thief has done but there is a need to throw him over the fucking side if they ever catch him.

According to the list on the shared drive, Jim reckons that, "You can't go around castrating people willy nilly," and "Dave has made his own bed so he will have to eat it." And as for Stuart, well when Jim heard that he won't be back for a while as he has got "Salamander poisoning." After taking the news in Jim then proclaimed that the whole thing "Sent his alarm bells flashing."

SUNDAY JULY 8TH

Bullshit bingo. I have been on a few jobs where the lads have almost lost the will to live and resort to bullshit bingo in management meetings. Basically it's a bingo card with all the buzzwords that get used. You just tick them off as you go and if you complete a card you have to let everyone in the meeting know. This is usually done by using the word 'bingo' in a statement you make or an answer you give. On here that would be too simple so we have resorted to phrases. Things like 'blue sky thinking', 'take ownership', 'the big picture', 'mission critical', 'low-hanging fruit', 'think outside the box' and 'get ahead of the curve'. I was one away from winning this morning. I only had the phrase 'park it' to go and none of the barnpots said it.

News just in: apparently Jim was on a tour of the cellar deck today and spotted one of the painters fannying about over an instrument stand. A ten-minute job had run to nearly an hour and Jim had watched every little repeated stroke, step back and inspection of admiration and touch up. In the end he lost it, went over to the guy and screamed, "For fuck's sake, you're not painting a Stradivarius!"

MONDAY JULY 9TH

Well Tony, the mate of little Geoff, brought the platform to a standstill today and it was all over tea breaks. The lads get a fifteen-minute tea break but obviously when you add in the time it takes to make the job safe and get to and from the tea shack that increases to thirty minutes. It's a norm and has never been a problem before but at this morning's break that all changed. Tony was shouting and bawling in the tea shack for the lads to get out before the break had been completed. Apparently the general foreman there, whose job it is to move people along, just stood open-mouthed. As they stood in shock the safety reps took over. Tony got the big fuck off and nobody budged an inch. It remained like that for two hours before an apology was given and the lads went back to work. If the management were in any doubt about the troop's feelings they were given another example at the afternoon break. The lads took one full hour and nobody said a word about it. Gobshite Tony was nowhere to be seen.

TUESDAY JULY 10TH

For the last week old Laurie the electrical construction engineer has been getting a hard time from Geoff to get the lighting and small power systems completed. Laurie has never lost his cool once and whenever it has been mentioned to him he just keeps replying by tapping the side of his nose. Today we found out why and it was absolutely brilliant. We were in the conference room which happens to be opposite the office of little Geoff. During the meeting a few of us watched as he returned to his office and wedged himself under the desk. We heard the winging and moaning and then one of the lads pointed out to the entire meeting that his desk was lower than all the others. That's when Laurie owned up. Each day for the last week he has been going into Geoff's office and sawing one quarter of an inch off each of the legs on his desk. On each occasion he also lowered his seat so that the ratio to the desk would remain the same. The whole meeting then sat and looked at short arse at his desk and it looked like a scene from a kindergarten. Well that was it, one person started to laugh and pretty so everyone in the room followed. Nobody could do a thing for the next thirty minutes. Short arse just kept giving us funny looks and each time he did it just made things worse.

WEDNESDAY JULY 11TH

Well the handover notes are written and the final shift is over. As I head back to the accommodation block with a head full of Kazakhstan I hear a familiar voice calling. Harry has cornered a newcomer and the cards are out. "Hey Andy, pick a card, any card you like." I don't know why I said it I just did. The words "The five of clubs" left my mouth in an instant. I will never forget the mesmerised look on the kids face as he looked down at the card in his hand and then across to me. He will learn soon enough I suppose.

THURSDAY JULY 12TH

Well it was my turn to say goodbye today. I have met a lot of fascinating people while working in this field and I hope to keep in touch with some of them. I left the platform with a proud sense of achievement and a bag full of CVs; after all, it's all about priorities.

TRIP EIGHT

WEDNESDAY JULY 25TH

My tickets arrived early morning and so did a kit bag full of PPE. It's all top of the range Helly Hansen stuff and to look at it you would think I was going to the North Pole. I checked the web once more and sure enough although the summers can get into the plus forties, the winters can get to the minus of the same degrees. I have never had to wear thermal underwear before but it looks like that will change before this year is out. No sooner had I packed it all away and the door bell rang. I got a registered letter from the agent to say that everything is off. I ring them and they just make some lame excuse about last minute changes. No sooner did the phone go down and it's back up again. It was another agent and they have taken over my contract. It's the same terms and conditions and so it's all back on again. Some last relaxing day at home this turned out to be. Thank God I had July 13th.

It was graduation day. My daughter Elizabeth had studied to be a primary school teacher at Sunderland University and she finally picked up her scroll at Sunderland's Stadium of Light. It was a proud day and the atmosphere, like the setting, was perfect. Elizabeth's achievement was best summed up by one guest speaker when she told a story about the crew of the Space Shuttle Challenger disaster. She remembered when they were introduced to the world and had to undergo the usual press conference. The seven crew members were each asked for their names and what they did in life.

"Dick Scobee, I'm an astronaut."

"Michael John Smith, I'm an astronaut."

"Judith Resnik, I'm an astronaut."

"Ellison Onizuka, I'm an astronaut."

"Ronal Ervin McNair, I'm a physicist."

"Gregory Jarvis, I'm an electrical engineer." Then all eyes turned on a thirty-seven year old bright-eyed, smiling lady from Concord, New Hampshire. "I'm Christa McAuliffe." she announced, "and I change the world." The stunned gathering was then told that she was a school teacher. What better way is there to describe such a noble profession?

THURSDAY JULY 26TH

I get the train from Darlington to Peterborough and then swap over for the train into Stansted Airport. At Cambridge a young lad got on, sat a few rows down from me and switched his portable music player on. That's when it began. Dumten, dumten, dumten, dumten. It was the usual boom box shite that some kids call music. The woman sitting across the aisle from me began to get more and more annoyed by the minute. In the end she just snapped. She got up and approached the kid. Dumten, dumten, dumten, dumten. She stuck a finger in his shoulder and screamed, "Are you deaf?" The kid looked up, took off his earphones, stopped his music and said, "Excuse me?" Dumten, dumten, dumten, dumten. The woman replied, "I said are you deaf?" Dumten, dumten, dumten, dumten. She then realised that the shite was still playing. The door and the end of the carriage slid open and she looked up to see a punk sat on the floor beyond it with a massive ghetto blaster. Dumten, dumten, dumten, dumten. She went bright red, apologised to the first kid and then went straight at the punk. Her screaming fit lasted for about five minutes. Our carriage had a good laugh at it all.

I met the agent's rep at the airport and handed him my medical certificate including an HIV test that I had to take. It's mandatory before they will let you in but it causes havoc with your GP. He doesn't want to sanction it as it sets off all kinds of alarm bells. Your name even goes on a register that various institutions like insurance companies can see. Anyway, with my docs in order he handed me a letter of introduction that I have to give in at the other end so that a visa could be put into my passport. The four-hour flight leaves at six, so I calculate ten o'clock plus four hours of time difference, giving me a local landing time in Uralsk of two am. They reckon two to three hours through Customs and then a two-hour bus ride to a camp we would be living on in the local town of Aksai. What was it Robert Frost once wrote?

> *I shall be telling this with a sigh.*
> *Somewhere ages and aged hence.*
> *Two roads diverged in a wood and I;*
> *I took the one less travelled by,*
> *And that has made all the difference.*

FRIDAY JULY 27TH

The project is running a chartered flight that begins in Italy, goes to the UK and then flies onto Kazakhstan. So when you get on the plane the first thing you have to do is move sleeping Italians. At Uralsk, a building has been set aside for the project so that Customs can give you special attention. You have to fill out a little piece of paper with all the valuables you are bringing into the country and it must include the amount of dollars you are taking in. It has to be exact as they count it out before you. Once you have shown your letter of invitation, obtained a visa and retrieved your battered case you then get to meet one of the six Customs officials. They check your little piece of paper and then proceed to go through every item in your case. The Italians try to short cut this by offering them a bottle of wine or perfume depending on who's doing the rummaging. I have already made my mind up in that they are getting nothing so we play the waiting game for a while. Eventually, I am allowed to get on one of the waiting buses. Overall the procedure is simple, if they don't like you then they put you back on the plane you came in on so you can leave with those people about to go on leave. If they are prepared to tolerate you then you can wait on a bus until the entire flight has been cleared and then you can rattle all the way to Aksai. Once there you get allocated a room on a Czech Camp situated on the edge of town. Three hours of sleep later you meet your new colleagues and undergo the usual safety inductions. As for the weather then it's in the thirties and so it's mad hot.

SATURDAY JULY 28TH

Today I found out just how big this project is. Karachaganak is a gas condensate field with an estimated reserve on 1.2 trillion cubic metres. On top of that it also has some 1 billion tonnes of liquid condensate and crude oil. Phase one of the project was all about making it safe to start work here. I am on phase two and it's said to be at a cost of four billion dollars. Some eighty-five existing wells are going to be reworked, existing primary separation facilities are going to be refurbished and new ones are going to be built. Over four hundred miles of pipeline are going in and several office and accommodation complexes are going to be built. Apart from building process facilities there is also a hearts and minds section to the project. We are going to be doing environmental remedial work thanks to a Soviet era of contamination. The legislation back then was non-existent so well blowouts and abandonment were commonplace. New investment means the building of roads, bridges, railways, water pumping and a 120MW gas-fired power plant to supply the project and local community with electricity. Maybe that's why there are over eleven thousand people employed on this project already.

The consortium that has been put together for it consists of British Gas, Chevron, Lukoil and Agip. So it's going to be a mix of Brits, Yanks, Russians and broken arrows. Out here the Italians are now known as broken arrows because they don't work and you can't fire them. Anyway, in between sorting out my new office I get to meet several Kazakh locals. They are warm friendly and I like them already. I was amazed at how they all knew my name and could hold a good conversation about where I had originated from. I found out the reason why at the end of the day. One of the first things you have to do in the site induction is fill out a form and get your picture taken so that you can obtain a security ID badge. The girl that does it also sends your details out to the people you are about to work with. Before I opened my mouth they knew all that there was to know about me.

SUNDAY JULY 29TH

Today is interview day and my new assistant is called big Yuri. He is studying to be lawyer, doesn't speak a word of English and spent fifteen minutes shaking like a leaf. After I had managed to calm him down through one of our interpreters we had a pleasant chat about what he wanted out of life. As a lawyer he could earn fifty dollars a month or he could come and work with me for six hundred dollars a month. That would mean a better home, a better life and if he stuck it then promotion through the ranks of the operating company. It had more of a ring to it than defending drunks and car thieves. The project did have English lessons for locals so I gave Yuri the job and put him straight on them. The bear hug he gave me almost broke me in two.

MONDAY JULY 30TH

As we were just finishing our first planning meeting Ian, our instrument engineer, noticed that one of the construction piping engineers was passing the office. He called him in and then winked to us all. "I need a colour off you, Peter."

"A colour! What for?"

"Well, you know Lynn in admin?"

"Yeah sure."

"Well we are conducting a survey on what colour her pubic hair is. Andy reckons black, Dave reckons blonde, Mike reckons..."

"You what? Are you insane?"

"Naw man, just have a guess and I will go and ask her." An argument went on for a good five minutes after which Peter blurted out the word 'brindle'.

"What the hell made you say that?" asks Ian.

"Well at home I have just had my drive blocked paved and the bricks chosen by the wife were brindle," he flustered.

"Brindle is orange and brown isn't it?" asked Ian. When Peter nodded Ian said it was a great answer and so he was going on the list. Peter just shook his head and left the room in a daze. We then sat in silence as Ian got Lynn on speaker phone. "Hello darling," he began "Have you got your dictionary at hand as I need some help."

"Fire away, Ian," she replied. "Peter has been in and he has tried to help me with my crossword but I think he has just made up a word. The clue is orange and brown colour. It's seven letters long, begins with a 'b' and ends with an 'e'. The word he gave was 'brindle' but I don't believe there is such a word." We hear the rustle of paper followed by, "I'm afraid he's right, Ian. Brindle can be orange and brown colouring." At this point we still didn't know what he was up to. Then it all became clear. "Do me a favour darling, will you pop your head into Peter's office and just say, 'Peter, you were right, it's brindle.' Don't say any more than that or he will gloat." It was brilliant. One minute later Peter came flying into the room and went berserk. He almost had a heart attack before Ian told him the truth.

TUESDAY JULY 31ST

It's pay day for the locals and as the banks usually run out of money the project has come up with a novel way of getting around it. All the locals go on a bus to town with the project money men. As they pay the salaries in the locals take it straight back out. Once back at work then it's time to make a little extra. You get asked to exchange your dollars for Tenge at a rate that is slightly less than the money exchangers in town. I'm not talking about companies here I'm talking about men on street corners with satchels of cash with an armed back-up not too far away. Anyway, once you do that they then exchange it back with them at the higher rate and so their salary for the month has just increased. It's a simple enterprise at its best and no-one minds doing it. The one thing you have to remember in all this is the 1993 rule.

When Kazakhstan broke away from Russia not only did the Russians destroy parts of the country's infrastructure, they also tried to ruin its economy. In 1993 the Russians flooded Kazakhstan with fake dollar bills that were all dated 1993 in hope of bringing the country to its knees. The Kazakhs are not that stupid and soon found out about it. Some notes did manage to get into circulation so even now the money men will not take any notes dated 1993 or before.

WEDNESDAY AUGUST 1ST

We had a team building night in the camp bar. The lads have discovered nectar from the gods. A local brewer has produced a beer by the name of 'Derbes' and it's as cheap as chips. Its fifty pence a bottle and hits the spot so let's just see how long it is before some local gangster takes the brewery over. It's good news all around apart from Slush Puppy Eddie, our electrical engineer. To explain, Hush Puppies are a very famous brand of footwear and Eddie wears them because they are comfortable on his bony feet. The thing is, as legend has it, when Eddie gets drunk he usually ends up pissing in them and so that's why he has acquired the name Slush Puppy.

It's not uncommon to go on a job and come across someone who has a tendency to piss in strange places after a night on the drink. The wardrobe tends to be the most common place. I once worked on a job in Heysham with a guy called Clive who used to piss the bed. He got a final warning once from the owner of the digs and so the next time he came in from the pub hammered he had the good sense to sleep on the floor. The trouble was that when some of the other lads found him they thought he had fallen out of bed and so they put him back in it. After he had managed to drag himself out of the shallow end the following morning he was thrown out on the street. He ended up renting a place in the end. I bet he never got much of his bond back when he let it go.

THURSDAY AUGUST 2ND

At the safety meeting today we all got the usual warnings about dehydration. Don't drink too much alcohol, do drink lots of water. Eddie just sat quietly and played in his puddles. We were shown a typical urine chart and advised that if your urine is bright orange then you are dehydrated and should stop work and take on water. If it's any of the other lighter shades shown then you can keep working but still have to keep taking the water. We are then shown the mosquitoes that will dine on us for the next few months and are advised to wear repellent. I have never used the stuff and never will for the simple reason it doesn't work. The room is already full of stinking expats covered in red craters to prove that. Some of the lads have brought out those electrified tennis racket things that make them light up and explode. The thing that gets me is the little black flies. When you are out in the field these things appear in their thousands. They don't sting or bite you they just bump into you. If you don't have a net over your head it ends up being like Chinese torture. If you do have one then it's only a matter of time before you can't see through it. Eddie never gets bothered by them, probably because they don't like the stink of piss.

FRIDAY AUGUST 3RD

Yuri is doing well and we need someone to work alongside him so it's interview time again. We had four people to do and I let Yuri sit in on them so he could have an input. With the first one we discussed pig farming and I learnt that there are more pigs in Kazakhstan than people. With the second it was all dental hygiene. With the third it was all about putting out a fire without destroying a building. So, on my note pad I had written pig farmer, dental assistant and fireman. Yuri and the interpreter were all smiles. When the fourth guy came in he introduced himself as Boris in a loud voice, sat down and answered all my questions in the same tone. Every fifth word was Kazakhstan and they were all delivered over my right shoulder. For the whole of the interview the guy never looked at me once. When he left I looked around to see if someone had sneaked into the room. Yuri and the interpreter were falling about laughing. When they eventually stopped the interpreter wrote 'news reader' on my pad. Apparently this guy worked for a regional TV station and every now and then he got to read news bulletins. Anyway Yuri rang Eduard the fireman and offered him the job.

SATURDAY AUGUST 4TH

When we Westerners do projects the paperwork has to conform to all the required standards and here it is no different. Where we have regulations, procedures and checksheets, they have GOST, SNIPs and AKTs. As no-one really knows what is required as of yet, the project has decided to do both. So today was all about taking the first step to becoming one of the project's so-called experts in both. It was the first time that I really had a chance to discover how these people had to work and how the Russians had such an influence on this country. They were told 'the big lie' as they call it and now they are doing things to put it right. They now know that they don't have the best standard of living in the world, that their possessions are the best that money can buy and that there is only one way to do a job and that is to document it to death. I hope the Kazakhs get to this part sometime soon. It's as if no-one dares deviate from what Stalin had put in place and it reminds me of a very famous myth with regard to the Trans Siberian Highway.

The TSH is the unofficial name for a series of highways that span the width of Russia. They run from the Baltic Sea of the Atlantic Ocean to the Japan Sea of the Pacific Ocean. There is an inexplicable semi-circular section that breaks the line of a particular segment and it has been put down to Stalin's finger. The myth is that Stalin used a rule on a map to show his engineers where the road had to go. The problem was that when he drew the pencil line it jumped around the area where his finger was on the rule. As the engineers were under strict orders to obey their leader and no-one dared question the route they never deviated from the drawing.

SUNDAY AUGUST 5TH

I have never seen such stupid working hours on a project like this before. The contractor works from 7am until 6pm Monday to Friday, 7am until 4pm on a Saturday and they don't work on a Sunday. Our construction team work from 7am until 6pm Monday to Saturday and on Sunday they do 7am until lunch time. I work for the commissioning team so we have to do 7am until 7pm every day. The reason is simple; one of our bosses is a British Gas staff clown, and he's Welsh. Some staffers are the same the world over when it comes to contract personnel like me. Yes, we are all one team but when it comes to timesheets, expenses and working hours then they turn into pantomime baddies. When you actually get into a commissioning phase then we work around the clock and don't mind that as that's what the job is all about. Right now we are still in the early phases of construction and they aren't even here on-site. We are all here on an empty site, well I say we, the Welsh clown isn't here but his spy is. That's another one of their little games. When they are not on-site they usually leave another staffer in charge whose main function is to report on anyone that leaves site before 7pm. Its childish I know, but it happens.

MONDAY AUGUST 6TH

There is a panic on. A canteen has been built at Unit 3 and someone has called for a working commission on Wednesday so that it can be approved and put in use on Thursday. I am given a car, a driver, a map and an interpreter and told to make sure that everything is in place. Firstly, I find out that a working commission is where government officials come to see if you have built something in accordance with their rules and regulations. If you have, they sign to say its ok, have a meal and everyone celebrates by getting pissed. If not you get a list of things to put right and the piss up gets put back until you do. Anyway, I had Oksana to help with language barriers and Bazergali to get us to and from them. I also remembered to take a small notebook so that I can start to throw away my ignorance. As far as I am concerned to get any sort of respect then I am going to have to learn Russian and a little bit of Kazakh. Russian is the main language used but this is Kazakhstan after all. After a hectic spell we had the required paperwork and I had my first few words.

Words.	Russian.	Kazakh.
Hello.	Preevyet.	Sarlem.
Good Morning.	Dobra Ootra.	Kairla Tan.
Good Afternoon.	Dobry Dyen.	Kairla Kun.
Good Evening.	Dobry Vaychir.	Kairla Kish.
Good Night.	Dobry Nochee.	Kairla Tun.
How are you?	Kak Dillar.	Kal Kali.
Fine, thank-you.	Hurushor.	Jacka.
Bye (Informal).	Paka.	Sowbol.

TUESDAY AUGUST 7TH

It's was my son's birthday today and amongst all the usual gadgets he found an odd toy. It was a toddler's red fire engine. When I rang to wish him all the best I had to tell him the history behind it. On one of his birthdays many moons ago I was clearing up the garden and he was riding around said fire engine. Half-way through the clear up the phone rang. Job stopped, gear off, front room, phone. "Hello?" I say.

"Hello," replies a voice "Can I speak to the owner of the property please as I have great deal on our new double glazing range."

"Hang on and I will get him." I then told Matthew, who had just learnt what a phone is, that someone wanted to speak to him. He toddled in and picked up the phone. He listened for a while and then calmly announced, "I have got a red fire engine." More silence was followed by "It's a big red fire engine." I moved onto the garden and fifteen minutes later he reappears. "Phone ok?" I ask. "Yeah, phone ok," he replies. About one hour later we retired for drinks and biscuits and I then noticed that he had not put the phone back correctly. As soon as I reconnect it the damn thing rang. "Hello?" said a familiar voice. "Did you know that because you left the line open I have not been able to make another call?"

"I have also got a red fire engine," I replied. "Do you want to hear about it?" He put the phone down and his company never bothered me again.

WEDNESDAY AUGUST 8TH

The working commission went well but was one of the strangest things that I have ever been involved in at work. Ten committee members turned up and each had their own little bit to sort out. The Fire Chief looked as the safety aspects of the building and according to Eduard he didn't like the type of fire extinguisher we had in place but he would help us change that later. His brother must have a shop somewhere. The sanitary and environmental officers were happy with the cleanliness and waste disposal, etc. so they spent most of the day outside smoking fags. The only awkward moment came when the state architect asked me why we only had forty coat hangers just inside the door when there was seating for two hundred people. I just couldn't believe what I was hearing. I told him that as it was summer not everyone brought a coat. "What about winter?" he asked. I just told him that when it got cold most people brought food into work and ate at their desks. It was nonsense but he just nodded and accepted it. Eventually, the big players got involved and all the documents were signed. The food soon disappeared and on the way to the camp bar I detoured out of the way. A few hours later I got a call to go back. When I got there I was handed a napkin with a note on it from the labour inspector. He had just worked out that the project expat to local employment ratio of 1:4 wasn't being met and needed something doing about it. I handed it to one of the managers and went to assure him that it would be looked into. I found him in the toilet throwing up the copious amounts vodka and orange juice he had managed to consume.

THURSDAY AUGUST 9TH

Yuri had his first English lesson and so afterwards we went over the alphabet. It took me back to when my children first learnt to speak. I soon realised that I was with an adult who was trying to learn a new language and it wasn't going to be easy for him. When I saw the effort he was putting in I was full of admiration for him. Through an interpreter I told him that we would read together every day and if ever there was anything that he didn't understand then he should stop me and I would sort it. In return he could help me with my Russian as I had just been told by the project that pond life like me don't qualify for Russian lessons. I joked that swear words were allowed but not in front of the girls "Fucking bastard smashing," he replied. I then heard Ian laughing through the office wall.

FRIDAY AUGUST 10TH

I got to spend a full day on the main process facility at KPC and took part in our first solid meeting with the contractor. They are an Arabic company by the name of Consolidated Contractors Company Saipem (CCC Saipem). They are the largest construction company in the Middle East and are in the top twenty international contractors. I sat next to their legislation expert called Fadi and it was he who took the minutes. He's a clever lad that was educated in Moscow and so he's fluent in Russian and his English isn't bad either. The only reason we chatted was that he noticed the few words that I had scribbled on my pad and praised me on my poor attempts to write in Russian. When I asked about the Arabic language he assured me that it was easy and if I ever wanted to learn then he had some good books I could use. He must be joking. I already knew that their words are written from right to left but their numbers are written from left to right so some documents have to be read from both sides at the same time. And when I say 'written' I mean rows of squiggly lines and dots that don't seem to have any spaces in between them. When it comes to Kazakh and Russian I will attempt to have a go but as far as Arabic is concerned I will just rely on the good old Western mixture of shouts and hand signals to get my point across.

SATURDAY AUGUST 11TH

I was informed by one of the managers today that they are going to be changing certain up and coming contracts for the locals. Instead of them getting full time contracts they are going to be put on a two-week on two-week off rotation. That means that the project can employ twice as many people at no additional monthly cost. The man from the labour ministry will be pleased.

Just as I went to file away the working commission documents for the canteen a woman by the name of Tatyana appeared at the door. She had been employed by the project to close out various actions from such commissions. Her first one wasn't even on my list. Apparently we had failed to show the members of the commission all the guarantees for the equipment in there. If we didn't come up with them then it could be a big problem. Four hours later and I had them all on my desk. Tatyana took one look at them and then informed me that they had to be in Russian. We were talking about things like a Morphy Richards kettle and a Russell Hobbs toaster. After telling her where to get off she closed the door and explained to me that if she had one thousand dollars then she could make the problem go away. I declined and then reported her to the management. I was then told that she was well-known as being a tricky customer and needed someone strong to watch over her and so as of Monday she's all mine.

SUNDAY AUGUST 12TH

It's Sunday so it's time to have a bit of culture. I have bought a book about Kazakhstan from a local shop and it's full of wonderful places and people. One such person was Abai Kunanbaev. He was born in 1845 at the bottom of the Chingiz Mountain in today's Abai district, located in Eastern Kazakhstan. He was a well-known Kazakh poet, thinker, composer, philosopher and the founder of written Kazakh literature. Here are some of his words:

The proof of the existence of one God, unique and omnipotent, is that for thousands of years people of different tongues have spoken of God, and, however many religions there might be, all consider that love and justice are the attributes of God. We are not demiurges, but mortals who know this world by the things created. We are the servants of love and justice. And we differ from one another in how well we comprehend the creations of the Most High. Believing and worshipping, we must not say that we can force others to believe and worship. The source of humanity is love and justice. They are omnipresent and decide everything. They are the crown of Divine Creation. Even the way a stallion takes possession of a mare is a manifestation of love. He who is swayed by the feelings of love and justice is a wise man and a learned man. Unable to invent science and learning, we can only behold and perceive the created world and understand its harmony by our reason.

He'll get no argument from me.

MONDAY AUGUST 13TH

Eduard and Tatyana have joined the team and a girl in our office has just turned eighteen so today I learnt a few customs. The first is to never shake hands across a door and the second is that I must never buy a girl a dozen roses.

When Eduard and Tatyana appeared at the office door with a member of security the first thing I did was to go over and offer them my hand. Rather than take it they both beckoned me to come forward. Not understanding what they meant I took a step back. They then crossed the door and shook my hand. Apparently unless you are both in the same room it brings bad luck.

When it was announced that Irina had turned eighteen I gave Yuri some money with the intention of getting her a box of chocolates and a dozen roses. He got the chocs and eleven roses. He then explained that for celebrations you traditionally buy odd numbers of flowers. You only buy even numbers for funerals.

A group gathered and then I learnt that you must not shake hands whilst wearing a glove (humiliation), never whistle indoors (you blow away your money), never buy anyone a watch (means you won't see them again), only cut bread with a knife (broken by hand means broken life), remove your shoes when entering someone's home (you will be offered slippers to keep the place clean), never refuse a drink or toast (bad etiquette) and if you leave the house but return immediately because you have forgotten something then you must make a slight change to your appearance (if not you will run into bad luck). When passing a cemetery, you must switch off any music and be silent and to remember those that have passed. I was then reminded about the bread people have been bringing into the office on a Friday. Apparently, this is done in memory of the dead and I have to say that Kazakh bread or Baursak as it is traditionally known is fantastic.

TUESDAY AUGUST 14TH

It's a hard life for the people here and you have to take your hat off to them. They never complain about it and are always there with a friendly smile in the morning. Aksai is an old town with Russian-style multi-coloured concrete apartment blocks added onto it. They are split by numeric regions with number ten having the des res bit. It may be simple and small but it has more heart and soul than some cities I have been in.

Today I learnt that the twenty-seven thousand residents only get water three times a day. It's on for two hours in the morning, two hours in the afternoon and two hours at night. That means that when it is on, families fill whatever they can so that it's available to use during the off times. On top of that each building has to pay an electricity bill at the end of each month. As the power is supplied from Russia then they are the ones who want the money. The only problem is that the amount that leaves the residents isn't the amount that gets to the Russians. So they convert the shortfall into days and switch off the power supplies for that amount of time. The sooner we get the pumping station and power plant up and the running then the better it will be all around.

I am spending more and more time on the Russian alphabet so that I can start to read words even if I don't exactly know what they mean. There are 33 letters, 21 consonants and 2 signs. There are five letters common to both English and Russian, seven look like English letters but have different sounds, thirteen are purely Russian but have familiar sounds and the rest need some getting used to. For example, they have a letter that sounds like the 's' in pleasure and another that sounds like the 'sh' in sheep.

WEDNESDAY AUGUST 15TH

Ramadan is the ninth month of the Islamic calendar and the observation of a month of fasting from dawn until sunset is regarded as one of the five pillars of Islam. Here at site the canteens open early so that people can eat and drink enough to see them through the day. The same canteens are also open late at night so they can also break their fast then. I tend to recognise and respect such a regime and so I never eat or drink in front of those that are observing it. That said today I saw one of the daftest things I have ever seen associated with it and it was all down to Brian, a safety officer at Unit 2. Brian is a Brit but somewhere in his history is a South African so Brian classes himself as one of them. There is a big flag on his office wall in an attempt to support this. He has also got himself an Arab wife and has promised her that he will stick to Ramadan… well in a fashion. I went to see him at lunchtime and when I opened his office door the lights were out and the curtains had been closed. Brian, the English South African, was at his desk stuffing his face with a sandwich. He screamed at me to hurry in and close the door and then went on to explain himself. He reckoned that Ramadan meant not eating when it was light but if it was dark then that was another matter altogether. I spent the next five minutes talking to this nutters silhouette before getting back to the real world.

THURSDAY AUGUST 16TH

I've added a few more words into my book and I keep going over them to make sure they stick.

Word	Russian	Kazakh
Thank-you	Spaseeba	Rachmet
Thank-you very much	Spaseeba Bolshoi	Kop Rachmet
You are welcome	Nyeh Za Sto	Kosh Kelderness
May I?	Morzhna	Ruskat Pa
Yes	Da	Yah
No	Nyet	Joch
Who	Kto	Kim
What	Shto	Ne
Where	Gdyeh	Kaida
When	Kagda	Kashan

Word	Russian	Kazakh
Which	Katory	Kai
Why	Puchimo	Nege
How	Kak	Kalai
You	Vay	Sien
Me	Mnyeh	Min
We	Meh	Bez

FRIDAY AUGUST 17TH

As we are not allowed to drive here we have a team of local drivers that have been allocated a car that they are allowed to take home of an evening. It seemed to be a fair arrangement until one of them fell asleep at the wheel this morning whilst bringing a few of the lads to work. It was a good job that the one sitting in the front seat had been alert as his quick reactions kept them all safe. When it was reported to the management a delegation went straight out to the driver's cabin to have a meeting. It took almost thirty minutes to awaken three of them. It then came to light that they have been putting the gift of a vehicle to use by using as a taxi at night. It's very rare for all the cars be put in use shortly after arriving on site as schedules need to be prepared and morning meetings need attending and the drivers know this. They have a rotation in place and those doing the taxi runs are at the bottom of it so that they can arrive at site and then catch up on lost sleep. It has now been decided that at the end of each shift the cars will be housed on the base camp and the drivers will get to and from work by a bus. It just goes to show you how a good deed can not only end up ruining it for all it can also put people's lives at risk.

SATURDAY AUGUST 18TH

According to the papers a certain society wants to make this 'bad poets day'. As I rate myself not bad in this category I would never dream of submitting one of mine to them. On the other hand my old school mate Keith would be in with a chance. I remember the day a miserable old English teacher of ours gave us a task to write one for our homework. I watched a game of football that night and wrote two passable verses about it. The following morning I delivered it to a quiet classroom. I got a small grunt of acknowledgement from old misery before giving way to Keith. He got to his feet and just stood there.

"Well?" bawled misery.

"Well what?" replies Keith.

"Poem lad, poem."

"Oh right," replies Keith as he rummages through his pockets to retrieve a crumbled piece of paper. After unravelling it he struck the pose and began. "The bog, by yours truly. I went to the bog, and out came a log, and my mother slapped me for not pulling the chain." As he sat down the whole place was in uproar. Misery went berserk, Keith got three lashes with a wooden cane and I got a moment that will live with me forever.

SUNDAY AUGUST 19TH

I have been finding more details about this incredible country. From east to west it stretches one thousand nine hundred miles. From north to south is stretches to one thousand miles. The length of its frontiers measures nine thousand three hundred miles, of which one thousand eight hundred are on water. With a total area of one million seven hundred thousand square miles then Finland, France, Greece, Italy, Portugal, Spain and Sweden would fit into its territory. It has fifty thousand lakes and eighty five thousand rivers yet many of its areas are still prone to drought. It has four climatic zones in wooded steppe, steppe, semi-desert and desert. Winters last four to five months, spring lasts one or two, summer lasts five and autumn gets what is left. Some of the world's most sought and endangered flora and fauna can be found here and this country really does have some pearls of nature. It's a shame that I will not be able to see much of it.

MONDAY AUGUST 20TH

I spent the morning meeting local people at the Unit 3 facility that exports gas and condensate to Orenburg and I thought it was a good time to learn how to say the days of the week in both Russian and Kazakh. While doing so I explained to our interpreters just how we got them. They never knew that it all started out as planets during the Roman Empire and when that collapsed the Germans and Scandinavians stuck their oars in.

Day.	Russian.	Kazakh.
Monday (Moon).	Punidyelneek.	Duisenbi.
Tuesday (Mars).	Ftorneek.	Bisenbi.

Day.	Russian.	Kazakh.
Wednesday (Mercury).	Sridar.	Sarsenbi.
Thursday (Jupiter).	Chitvyairk.	Sisenbi.
Friday (Venus).	Pyatnitsa.	Zhuma.
Saturday (Saturn).	Sooborta.	Senbi.
Sunday (Sun).	Vuskrisyaynya.	Zheksenbi.

TUESDAY AUGUST 21ST

A few of the team have set up a charity committee here and I have been asked to join. Because I am ok on the quiz front and can produce the odd funny PowerPoint show they want me to fill the gaps between some talented people. Bands have been put together and singers have been roped in to help with it all. One of my first tasks was to go and see a few worthy causes. This region has some 539 daily comprehensive schools, seven specialist and four higher education institutes. I went to a local school to meet the headmistress and some of the children. Books and stationery weren't a priority as shoes were. When I was told how many children attended the school I couldn't work out how they all managed to fit in. I then learnt that as there isn't any money to build schools, the children in the area are educated on a shift system. It's like having two schools in the one building. The first school attend from 7.00am until 13.00pm and the second from 13.00pm until 19.00pm. Some of the teachers cover both shifts.

WEDNESDAY AUGUST 22ND

Part of the on-going upgrades at the Unit 3 plant include the gathering of low pressure vaporized gas instead of sending it to flare, the gathering and recycling of water-methanol mixture, improved management of processing trains due to new air compressors and air dehydration devices for instrumentation and automatic systems as well as the enhancement to existing safety systems. With the latter in mind the question on everyone's lips was, "There has to be a firewater line here somewhere." That's what the civil team were saying while digging holes all over the Unit. The project had done an on-site upgrade and they needed to tie it in to a certain point in the existing system. The only problem they had was that the buried pipe was not as per the as-built drawings. They had been digging for days with no joy so it was check all the documentation time. After a few hours in the local archive I found what we were looking for. It was the original workpack for the upgrade which dated back to the Russian era. The additional drawings gave us no clues but the list of people that worked on it did. Old Sergei was still on the project and he was still at Unit 3 so we went to see him. He remembered the job and the Russian soldiers that were guarding them at the time. They were told that once the work had been completed they were all going to work on a pipeline in Siberia. Not wanting any of that the engineers bamboozled the military with a lot of civil jargon and so the firewater system just got longer and longer. The plan worked and as no-one wanted to tell the authorities what had gone on so the drawings remained as is. Sergei reckoned the soldiers had eventually worked out what was going on and as they didn't want to leave either they turned a blind eye to it all. Anyway, Sergei redlined the drawing for us from memory and within a few hours the construction team found their required section of pipe.

THURSDAY AUGUST 23RD

I mentioned the school to the lads in the office and told them that we hope to help them with one of the charity nights. Word got around and before the shift was over we had donations that amounted to eight hundred dollars. We rang the school and then sent someone down with the money. Later on, in the bar, we got word that the children were over the moon with their new shoes. It just goes to show you how wonderful human nature can be at times. One minute it's column filler and the next it's a headline. There are some great people here.

FRIDAY AUGUST 24TH

I learnt a valuable lesson today. Never ask the same question to an Indian and a Pakistani when they are standing right next to each other. I had to get the As-Built status of the drawings on the potable water system and Samit and Rashid were in charge of them. So picture the scene as I walk into their office and ask the question. Without saying a word they both began to nod their heads. It was like watching those little dogs people have on the dashboard of their cars. Their heads were rolling in all directions. "Just say something!" I screamed. I then got a "Yes, Mr Andy." and a "No, Mr Andy." That's when war broke out. Both thought that they were in charge and so were constantly trying to outdo each other and it showed. The screaming began and I stood there until my ears couldn't take anymore. I left them to sort it out and Yuri eventually got the drawings.

SATURDAY AUGUST 25TH

Young Tommy, the graduate from operations, is the sort of person that would look shite in a million dollar suit. Anyway he's young, free, and single, has pockets of cash and easily gets pissed. It's no wonder then that he got himself a girl last night and it's no wonder he was in the bar with us tonight telling us how horribly wrong it all went. Once he was back at her place she stripped him down and poured him a whisky. He drank it and when offered another he couldn't say no. After a few moments of sitting alone he went in search for the girl. When he looked in the bathroom he saw the bath full of water and thought that she had prepared it for him. So what does Drunken Tommy do? He climbs in and waits. When the girl found him she went absolutely berserk. Her next few washes and cups of tea were now going to have a hint of his sweaty bollocks on them. He never knew about the water rationing the locals had to endure. When we asked him about how cold the water must have been he assured us that it wasn't that bad. Yeah right, and as for the money! Well she screamed long enough and hard enough for him to hand it all over.

The charity committee have booked the main bar on the camp for Tuesday 28th so the pressure is on. I have an idea but it needs a disc bringing out and I will need the help of a good, long-haired dictionary or perevodchik (interpreter).

SUNDAY AUGUST 26TH

According to Greek and Persian written sources of the first century BC this land used to be full of nomadic tribes known as 'Saks' and 'Turs'. A century later and a Great Silk Road later the Kangyus turned up. A further two centuries on and Atilla the Hun swept across the nation with his barbarous hordes. After that there was an Arab conquest and Islam was introduced to the nation supported by the Karakhanid and Karakhitais dynasties. By the twelfth century the Kypchaks attempted to unionise the country and at the beginning of the thirteenth century Genghiz Khan appeared. Backed by the Turks he took the Mongols on a bloody conquest that removed some places from the world map forever. Otrar, the then cultural centre of southern Kazakhstan, was one of them. The nation didn't recover until the Kazakh Khanate was formed in the fifteenth century. They now had a national identity and it would remain that way until a certain nation had other ideas. The Red Empire was on its way and so is the disc I need for the show.

MONDAY AUGUST 27TH

Whenever you go to handover a system to an operator one of the things you must do is make sure that all the vessels in that handover have undergone an internal inspection before the lids have been closed. The Kazakhs use a 'passport' system which is a dedicated dossier that contains all the inspection criteria and supporting manufacturing data. The only problem we have with it is that the regulations for vessels are in conflict with each other on material, pressure, size and use. So today I went to see Nurlan, the local expert, and took Yuri with me. I only needed the answer to one question – what is a vessel? I handed over all the confusing regulations, and before long a scrum had formed in his office. I sat patiently for nearly an hour before getting the answer I needed. Nurlan stood in front of me and opened his arms like a lying fisherman. He then swung them in a circular direction before coming back to the original position. So that was it. A lifetime of engineering and regulation had all came down to this wooden head and his reach. I was that pissed by it all I walked over to him, put my finger tips against his and then proceeded to leave the room with my arms open. I did remember to turn sideways as I walked through the door. It was a good job I wasn't driving.

I have finished the PowerPoint and I received the disc. We just had time for one rehearsal before calling it a day.

TUESDAY AUGUST 28TH

The day was all about commissioning telecoms (phones and radios) and the night was all about the show. The bar had some four hundred people in it and everyone had a great time. The band was spot on and the expat and local singing talent was excellent. In between it all we did 'Who Wants to be a Millionaire' on the big screen and we had the music from the show blasting out over the speakers. I was doing Tarrant's job with a laptop and the atmosphere could not have been better. I arranged for four of the managers to take part and for a laugh I set them up. They would get a sensible question on-screen and if they answered it correctly it was then followed by daft one that was associated with them. Chris, one of the gaffers from Unit3 plant opened with the question: Which of the following movies did not include Charles Bronson? Was it A: The Great Escape, B: The Magnificent Seven, C: Kelly's Heroes or D: The Dirty Dozen. He correctly answered 'C' and so the next question that came up on screen was: When you got pissed last Thursday which of the following people did you spew up over A: Bob, B: John, C: Dave or

D: Rab. He just cringed and the bar was filled with laughter. It went like that with all four of the managers and they all participated well. At the end of the night we had collected around five thousand dollars. It was a good start and it was all down to those that put in the time and contributed.

WEDNESDAY AUGUST 29TH

We went to the bar outside the local Tnarva (Mall) for a mid-week dust buster and witnessed the first deportation in the making. The bar only has one toilet and the queues can get quit long so it pays to keep your wits about you. Anyway, our compressor vendor left it until his bladder was about to burst before making a move. After a while in the queue he suddenly had 2000 psi at the end of his knob and he was left with no choice but to release it. He ran around the corner of the bar to relieve himself and unlucky for him two policemen were watching. Now these guys don't need much of an excuse to get rid of an expat and he had just played right into their hands. An attempted bribe failed as a deportation meant promotion and the name in lights. The vendor was taken off to jail and we were advised by the locals that he would be leaving on the next available flight.

THURSDAY AUGUST 30TH

The vendor has left. The deportation stamp in his passport bars him from entering Kazakhstan for one calendar year. I am sure it will take some explaining to his company and the wife. I know which is going to be the easier of the two.

Two of our lads used to work in Tengiz and they told us today that they were sacked for being over the limit on their way to work. Apparently, down there the camp security guards used to make a note of guys walking home pissed at night so that they could test them in the morning. For everyone they caught they got paid a bonus. The only problem was that so no-one could be seen to be singled out they tested everyone in the associated car. The two lads with us were unluckily sharing the car of one guy that had been fingered. They had spent a quiet night in with a few bottles but ended up in the trap.

FRIDAY AUGUST 31ST

Every time I now see Viktor one of our local electrical engineers he greets me with, "Smee again." It has to do with a joke I told him last week and it's still at the top of his funny list.

A radio station is having a competition whereby you can win a holiday if you can come up with a word that is not in the English dictionary but it sounds ok in a sentence. Dave rings in with the word 'Gaan'. When the DJ confirms that it's not in the book and asks him for the sentence, Dave, who is live on air, says, "Gann fuck yourself." After five minutes of silence the DJ comes back and apologises and reminds everyone that it's a live show and such language will not be tolerated. He then asks for the appropriate spirit to be used when ringing in. The competition continues and thirty minutes later Bob rings in with the word 'Smee'. The DJ confirms that it's not in the book and when he asks him for the sentence he hears, "Smee again, gaan fuck yourself."

SATURDAY SEPTEMBER 1ST

Today I was back onto my Russian and it was the months of the year.

Month.	Russian.	Kazakh.
January	yeen-VAHR'	Kantar
February	fee-VRAHL'	Akpan
March	mahrt	Nauryz
April	ah-PRYEHL'	S{ae}uir
May	mahy	Mamyr
June	ee-YOON'	Mausym
July	ee-YOOL'	Shilde
August	AHV-goost	Tamyz
September	seen-TYAHBR'	Kyrk{yu}yek
October	ahk-TYAHBR'	Kazan
November	nah-YAHBR'	Karasha
December	dee-KAHBR'	Zheltoksan

SUNDAY SEPTEMBER 2ND

I have been looking into the Russian question and it seemed to have taken off in the seventeenth century when Russian traders and Cossacks began to appear on the northern borders of Kazakh territories. Before long the tsarist government began to strengthen its influence by building towns and increasing the fortifications there. Battles raged and eventually the authority of the Khans was reduced. Colonial oppression, higher taxes, landlord wealth and feudal exploitation soon followed.

Lands were seized and due to overpopulation in certain areas peasants were moved en mass to the southern regions. The country couldn't take it and people began to starve. In 1916 when the Tsar attempted to conscript Kazakhs into the Russian imperial army, a revolt began. It was brutally suppressed and thousands of Kazakhs were killed. Many of those that survived fled to China and Mongolia. Of the few that remained some attempted to set up an independent national government but those involved were caught and executed. A few years later, Kazakhstan was under the control of the Soviets and it would remain that way until 1991.

MONDAY SEPTEMBER 3ʳᴅ

All railways in this country are built by Russian company by the name of TKA. This morning I saw a sample of how they work and it's fascinating. It's the first time I have ever seen a train carrying its own track and then putting it into place as it moves along. The team associated with it are very efficient and they are a happy sing-a-long lot. My main reason for seeing them was to do with a hold up on a section of track which was going to run into our main production facility at KPC. Their chief engineer assured me that it would be sorted soon as he was just waiting for the local Akim (Mayor) to sort a few local farmers out. He then produced a drawing to show me what the problem was. The track ran across four different farm lands and in accordance with the law each owner had to be paid an agreed sum of money to allow TKA to do it. Anyway, the four farmers in question each divided their land into four different strips and reregistered them all with family members. It now meant that TKA would have to make sixteen payments instead of four. As they were not prepared to do it they got in touch with the Akim. Apparently he was going to give them twenty-four hours to change it back or he was going to take all their land off them. One thing for sure, this place doesn't lack enterprise, even misplaced enterprise at that.

TUESDAY SEPTEMBER 4ᵀᴴ

You can get tins of Beluga caviar here for about five pounds. The same tins at home would cost you three hundred pounds. You are allowed to take ten of them home. As usual I was asked to take some through but I just declined. I have got three tins so that I can let a few people at home sample it. I have tried it and I honestly can't see what all the fuss is about. Believe me when I say that the name might be special but the product would take a lot of getting used to.

WEDNESDAY SEPTEMBER 5TH

We just couldn't understand what was going on. Although the work at the water pumping stations wasn't fully complete the systems had been commissioned and so water was available to the town twenty-four hours a day. That's not the case according to the locals as they were still on the three times a day routine. When the management took it up with the local authorities they were told that they were going to phase it in gradually. Apparently when water was short some residents would bleed it out of radiators. That meant that some piping joints would not be secure and so some apartment blocks could get flooded. There was also concern about the systems as a whole as they have never had a constant supply of water running through them. I think sometimes it's just better not to ask.

THURSDAY SEPTEMBER 6TH

I never drink alcohol when I travel to and from work. I rest before I set off and once I'm moving I tend to stick to soft drinks, a good book and my latest music. As I was standing in the queue at Uralsk airport, waiting my turn to be messed around by Customs, I was forced to watch drunken Chris and his 'Someone has taken my passport routine'.

The bus journey from the camp to the airport began at 2.00am. Chris spent the six hours before that getting pissed in the camp bar. He then dashed back to his room to get changed and pick up his case. He spent the entire journey to the airport in a comatose state. When he eventually awoke his hair was stuck up all over the place and the bus seats had creased their way into his face.

The guy at the Customs desk just looked up and shook his head before politely saying, "Passport." Chris then delves into the pocket of his baggy-arsed tracksuit bottoms and finds nothing. After a mild panic the Customs guy points to his other pocket. Chris attempts to put his hand in but can't quite manage it. He then realises that he has the bottoms on back to front and proceeds to take them off and turn them around. As we all look on in horror he then finds the passport and hands it over. The Customs guy took it between thumb and forefinger and just stamped it. He then asked Chris to show him the contents of his case. Chris heaves it onto the desk and goes flying over the top of it. As the table collapses the Customs guy falls back over his chair. Anyway, when the screaming and shouting eventually stopped, Chris opened an empty case. He had forgotten to pack it and so when he went to lift it he was expecting there to be some weight in it. What a way to end the first trip.

Trip Nine

Thursday September 20th

I went to a sportsman's dinner a few nights ago in Middlesbrough and the guest speaker was Liverpool football legend Tommy Smith. His stories were superb and my favourite was to do with the welsh winger Leighton James. Tommy told us how he was being ribbed in the press by James on what he was going to do to him on Saturday. The lads in the dressing room made sure the press clippings were everywhere. Come match day Tommy had made up his mind that he would put him in his place early on in the game. Five minutes in and the ball goes out of play. Tommy picks up the ball and who is going to take the throwing but James. "Come down this wing this afternoon and I will break your back," Tommy snarled. A shaken James took the throw and disappeared somewhere across the pitch. Five minutes later and Tommy has kicked someone up in the air and a free kick is given. Who steps forward to take it, Leighton James. As the referee approaches Tommy warns the Welshman, "Remember what I said, you come down this left wing and I'm going to break your back." A concerned James then turns to the ref and asks, "Did you hear that?"

"Every word," he replies.

"And what are you going to do about it?"

"Fuck all," began the ref. "But if I was you I wouldn't go down this left wing."

It seems like a lifetime away now as I'm standing at the exchange desk at Stansted explaining to the girl that the dollar bills I need have to be dated after 1993 because of Russian forgeries. It doesn't seem like five minutes ago that I arrived home to hear people saying things like, "My, that was a quick trip," or, "When are you going back then?"

FRIDAY SEPTEMBER 21ST

We had a visit from President Nursultan Nazarbayev today. It started by the clearing of all the roads. Then certain people were told to go home. Then a big letter 'H' was quickly placed in the secured area of the materials yard. That was followed by the arrival of uniforms and suits everywhere. Eventually, two identical helicopters appeared. I suppose it was so that would-be terrorists would have to fire two missiles instead of one. Anyway, both landed without incident and the President appeared before the line of selected dignitaries. In keeping with tradition, two beautiful girls dressed in traditional costume were there to offer him bread and salt to which he happily accepted. Hands were shaken, photographs were taken and then it was off to the front area of the main office block. A clear piece of pipe had been set up with a dummy valve handle. The President stood before it, made a wonderful speech about getting oil and then proceeded to turn it. The nod was given and the two lads behind the office switched a portable pump on. The oil ran through the temporary hoses, across the clear section of pipe and back into the drum it had come from. The cameras rolled, the gathering crowd cheered and a very enthusiastic reporter puffed out his chest and began to go slightly over the top with our glorious achievement. One hour later everything was back to normal and we were still nowhere near to producing any oil.

SATURDAY SEPTEMBER 22ND

I went to see the boys on the gas export pipeline today, just to make sure we are all completing all the same documentation for the authorities. Whilst I was there they showed me what they were doing and pretty soon the Russians are in for a shock. When they ran this country they always made sure that every export pipeline had a section that ran on their soil. That way they could always have a say in what happens. Well according to the drawings I saw today the ones exporting the gas are being rerouted so as they don't touch Russian soil. Once the new sections are complete the project will reroute the gas and so the section of pipe on Russian soil will see nothing. No wonder Putin wants to be friends with Kazakhstan again.

SUNDAY SEPTEMBER 23RD

To some he was a hero and to others he was a villain. He was born in 1878, died in 1953 and in between that time became one of the biggest mass murders the world has ever known. He began life as Ioseb Besarionis dze Dzhugashvili but like most Russian revolutionaries he changed his name. Ulyanov became Lenin, Bronstein became Trotsky and Skryabin became Molotov and so Dzhugashvili eventually became Stalin. The so-called man of steel was General Secretary of the Soviet Union's Communist Party and his purges claimed the lives of millions.

There is a village in northern Kazakhstan by the name of Dolinka and its cemetery is full of ethnic Germans and other various deportees that were deported from the Soviet Union so that they could perish in a labour camp. It wasn't the only one; they stretched from Russia's arctic tundra all the way to the Kazakh steppe. In Dolinka there are morbid bouquets of barbed wire and the odd crumbling barrack to remind people of the past. It is estimated that between 1.5 and twenty million people lost their lives in the gulag camps. History has shown that Stalin led one of the biggest crimes against humanity and yet in Russia he is still regarded as one of the most popular people in history.

In Kazakhstan you can see that they are still struggling to come to terms with all this. The Kazakhs are a kind, gentle and forgiving people and although you do hear of the odd protest here and there, in the main no-one ever broaches the subject. They have built a museum at Dolinka and its walls are covered with a pictorial tragedy that every child of this great nation should be made aware of. Maybe if they learn about what had happened back then they could do what is right by their elders. It's all right to forgive but it's even better to remember.

MONDAY SEPTEMBER 24TH

A few of the locals have seen my interest in history and we had a discussion about Stalin today. They told me that some parents adored him but others just despised him. During it all they asked me about Winston Churchill. I told them that the majority of people loved him but some had good reason not to. He had many great words and moments and I told them one of my favourites. It was when he received Sergeant James Allen Ward at 10 Downing Street to congratulate him on receiving the Victoria Cross. In 1941 Ward was in a Wellington bomber over the North Sea when the starboard engine caught fire. Even though the plane was 13,000 feet above the water he tied a rope to his waist and wing walked to extinguish the flames. Ward was a nervous wreck in front of the great man. Churchill noticed it and whispered, "You must feel very humble and awkward in my presence." After a moment the young hero managed to say, "Yes." Churchill simply replied. "Then let me tell you how humble and awkward I feel in yours."

TUESDAY SEPTEMBER 25TH

Alan, one of our electrical engineers came in for a chat today and it was all about his team Manchester United. He had been to a few games when he was off and he met Nobby Stiles. I then told him about the sportsman's dinner I went to during my leave and also about one I once went to where the guest speaker was Paddy Crerand. He was great entertainment and I managed to remember two of his stories about Nobby Stiles. Paddy wasn't present at the first as it was October 1960 and Nobby was making his debut for Manchester United against Bolton Wanderers. The manager, Matt Busby, gets the little fella in the middle of the dressing room in front of the team. He tells him that if they win he will get a bonus and then asks him what he would do with it. Nobby tells him that he would give it to his mother. Busby then tells him that there are eleven players out on that pitch wanting to steal it from his mum. With fire in his eyes Nobby runs out and warms up. One minute before kick-off he crouched down to tighten his bootlaces. As is tradition, the Bolton skipper comes over to wish him all the best in his career. Nobby looks him straight in the eyes and shouts, "Fuck off, you robbing bastard."

It's August 1970 and Manchester United are at home to rivals Leeds United. Nobby has constantly been dropped in pre-season games by manager Wilf McGuinness so he's determined to play his heart out. Ninety minutes later and Leeds have won the game by a single goal. The only person that had a good game was Nobby. The manager walks into a quiet dressing room and starts to ask the players about their performance. "I thought I did well enough with the amount of ball I saw," said Charlton. "I could not have covered another yard," said Kidd. Paddy Crerand looks to Nobby and sees him get angrier by the word. "All my shots were on target, the keeper had a blinder," said Best. Then the manager turned to Nobby. "Well it's obviously all my fucking fault isn't it?" he screamed. "Every fucker else has had a blinder so it must be me." McGuinness walked quietly over to the door and before leaving said, "Nobby you are dropped."

WEDNESDAY SEPTEMBER 26TH

I went to a start-up meeting at Unit 2 today and it began in a strange fashion. As we were about to discuss a new build on virgin soil then a sacrifice had to be made. A crowd had gathered and the centre of attention was some poor old sheep. Prayers were said and then before you knew it the sheep had its throat cut. Everyone stood in silence as it did the dance of death and its blood graced the soil. It's not something you want to see first thing on a morning but certain protocols have to be observed and they are best done so in a dignified silence.

THURSDAY SEPTEMBER 27TH

I learnt my numbers today and they are as follows: 1 adeen, 2 dva, 3 tree, 4 cheetyre, 5 pyat, 6 shest, 7 sem, 8 voseem, 9 deveet, 10 deseet, 11 adeenatsat, 12 dveenatsat, 13 treenatsat, 14 cheetyrnatsat, 15 peetnatsat, 16 sheesnatsat, 17 seemnatsat, 18 vaseemnatsat, 19 deeveetnatsat, 20 dvatsat, 30 treetsat, 40 sorak, 50 peejsyat, 60 sheejsyat, 70 semeestyat, 80 voseemeesyat, 90 deeveenosta, 100 sto, 200 dvestee, 300 treesta, 400 cheetyreesta, 500 peetsot, 600 sheessot, 700 seemsot, 800 vaseemsot, 900 deeveetsot, 1000 tyseecha.

FRIDAY SEPTEMBER 28TH

Someone has had the bright idea to put us all through our local driving test so that we can drive our own vehicles. I took my test just before lunch; it lasted twenty minutes and passed by without any dramas. I actually spent more time filling out forms and having my picture taken than I did in the actual car. By the end of shift I was then informed that it had all been a waste of time. The project drivers had worked out that if we get to drive the cars then there would be no need to employ as many of them as we do. The right people got to hear of it and before you knew it the tests were cancelled and those of us that had been given a local licence had to hand them back in.

SATURDAY SEPTEMBER 29TH

I had an accident today. While inspecting a camp that was being built to house project personnel I tripped over. When my hat came off my head hit some rebar and the blood began to pour. I jumped in the car and set off to see the Unit 3 doctor. Thirty minutes later he shaved my head, stuck on a patch and told me that I needed stitches. Forty minutes later I am back in the Czech camp clinic with two doctors fighting over me. One is Dutch and the other is a Brit. It's been a while since they had something of interest to do so they both want to do it. As I sit on the bed with my head thumping they can't find any anaesthetic. "Do it without," I say.

"But it will hurt," they say.

"It's bloody hurting now," I reply. Anyway the cloggy gets to do the stitches and the Brit gets to sulk. As soon as it's over I get up to go back to work but they say that I have to stick to the rules and have the rest of the afternoon off. I radio it in and then go to walk back to the billet. That's a no-no also, as I have to go in the ambulance. The fact that I can walk it in two minutes has got nothing to do with it. It took them both twenty minutes to find the ambulance driver and a further fifteen minutes for him to get it to work. He then drives the long way around the camp because he doesn't get to do it that often. At midnight there is a knock on my door and I awake and open it to the two doctors who want to know if I have managed to get some sleep.

SUNDAY SEPTEMBER 30TH

In the 1980s after a period of economic, political and social stagnation the Soviet Union began to collapse. Perestroika, or restructuring, was introduced and brought new hope but it was short-lived. The authoritarians in Moscow began to send out contradictory signals and in the December of 1986 a mass demonstration by young Kazakhs in Almaty ended in tragedy. Several people were killed and many demonstrators were either beaten or detained without just cause. The unrest grew and in 1990 Kazakhstan declared its sovereignty as a republic. After the failed coup in Russia the following year Kazakhstan declared its independence on 16th December 1991. It was the last of the soviet republics to do so. A new journey had begun and President Nursultan Nazarbayev was the man chosen to map its course.

As it stands Kazakhstan now has fourteen provinces which are sub-divided into districts. Each province is governed by a provincial Akim who oversees numerous municipal Akims. In 1997, the old capital of Almaty was changed to that of Astana. More friends are being made and more oil companies are turning up. There is a lot of wealth being generated here – I just hope that some of it eventually finds its way to the right people.

MONDAY OCTOBER 1ST

I had to go and see Brian, the Ramadan-following South African, again today about an issue on safety and I was glad to see that he had managed to come through his ordeal. It can't have been easy for him eating in a darkened office while the sun shone so brightly outside. He had lost weight during Ramadan and so his wife now wants him to keep his trimmed down figure. That's when he opened his desk drawer and showed me a sandwich box with five little silver foiled packages in it. They were in order as each of them had the days of the week printed on them. I thought it was some kind of bizarre calendar but there was an even stranger reason behind it. So that he didn't have to go to the canteen each day and succumb to the array of delights there she had made him a set of sandwiches for the week. She would have done one each night but she just couldn't be arsed so she prepared the lot on a Sunday. I never bothered to ask what Friday's tasted like but I did ask about Saturday and Sunday. Apparently they were his holidays and so he could eat whatever he wanted. I got away from him as fast as I could and as I left the car park I saw the strangest of things. One of the dogs from site was negotiating his way through some silver foil and Brian was heading for the canteen. The things you see when you don't have a gun.

TUESDAY OCTOBER 2ND

I have been roped into doing a quiz night for charity. They have had them in the past but when the old quiz master left the job nobody could be arsed to take it on. I offered to do one and they obviously like this stuff out here as the bar was packed. I kept to a simple format. It was quick joke, open with sports questions, have various rounds for general questions, song lyrics, name the year and pictures. To end each quiz it was one of those questions that got people talking the next day.

The opening joke: there are three old men in a doctor's waiting room. The first is sixty, the second is seventy and the third is eighty. A nurse appears and asks them what is wrong. "I get up at six every morning," says the first. "I stroke it, pull it and twist it but it still takes me thirty minutes to have a small pee." The nurse nods and turns to the second. "I get up at six-thirty every morning, I push, squirm, twist and squeeze my head but it still takes me thirty minutes to pass a small stool." The nurse nods again and moves to the third. "At six every morning I piss like a racehorse and at six-thirty I shit like a cow." "Then why are you here?" asks the nurse. "Because I don't wake up until seven," he replies.

There were lots of sports fans in so I hit them with one hell of an opening question on football. Who won the First Division title most times between 1970 and 1980 and who was runner up most times for the same period? Most got the first part straight away as it was Liverpool. They had won it five times. The second part of it had everyone beat. Most teams put Leeds United as they won it twice. The actual answer was Liverpool again as they were runners up on three occasions. I could have used the time period from 1970 to 1990 as the answer to that is also Liverpool and Liverpool.

To name the year I gave the following clues: The United States boycotted the Olympics in Moscow, Michael Foot became leader of the Labour Party and in The TV show Dallas, J.R Ewing got shot, British Leyland launched its new Metro and John Lennon was murdered. All that happened in the year of 1980.

For the last question I asked the teams: If you write down all the numbers from zero to one hundred on a piece of paper, how many times would you write the number nine. The usual dunces wrote eleven and got it wrong. The actual answer is twenty as many people forget some of the nines in the ninety series.

WEDNESDAY OCTOBER 3RD

Once again Chris got pissed last night so the first thing he did this morning was to bark at his manservant Steve to go and get him a cup of coffee. You sometimes see that in this game where a guy gets someone a job and expects him to do it as well as completing the odd chore. Anyway, Steve runs around after Chris and this morning he has a big problem. Chris likes lots of milk in his coffee and we have just run out. Replacements are on the way but Chris will need a hot drink before then. Steve is now standing in the kitchen and the panic button has been well and truly pressed. With Chris's voice booming in the background Steve searches high and low. He stops when he sees the cat in the corner licking up his breakfast. Chris's voice gets louder so Steve takes the milk off the cat and pours it into Chris's coffee. As he scampered out of the kitchen the cat began to wash itself, maybe it knows more than we do.

THURSDAY OCTOBER 4TH

Some of the girls from the agent's office in the UK are out here on a visit and today we took them to the market so that they could buy some music CDs. Whilst we were there a girl called Karen stood next to me as we watched to farmers haggle over a pig. They were locked in a handshake and the exchange just got louder and louder. Eventually a bargain was struck and said pig was picked up by the back legs and dragged to a nearby car. The boot was opened and the pig was unceremoniously thrown in. The boot was closed and then the pig tried in vain to smash its way out of it. Karen began to cry and said, "He is going to eat that, isn't he?" Well if he was going to play hide and seek with it that would have lasted too long so I suppose eating it was the next best thing. I never said anything; I could have mentioned the sheep from Unit 2 but thought better of that as well.

FRIDAY OCTOBER 5TH

Here at KPC the facility will handle production through infield flowlines from producing wells in the field as well as taking care of the unsterilized hydrocarbons from Unit 2 and Unit 3. There are three condensate treatment trains here that have associated sour gas and fuel gas sweetening treatment facilities. The condensate gets stabilised, sweetened and exported via a newly-built export pipeline. The sour gas is dehydrated and controlled for gas reinjection or export to Orenburg whilst some is sweetened for use as fuel gas. The three trains here come under our system champion, Jeff from Bolton, but right now his coat is on a shaky nail. For weeks now he has been banging on about some expenses that he got rejected during a vendor visit he did in the UK. He went as part of a factory acceptance test (FAT) and basically he took the piss. He used first class travel and some of the meals he had would have meant that he must have eaten his own body weight at each sitting. It was obvious that he wasn't a table for one but he still expected to get fully reimbursed for it. Well today that all came to a head. He sent the agent a final ultimatum and along with a copy of his contract and asked them to invoke the highlighted clause 23 with regard to the approval of expenses. The agent must have been pissed as all they did was return it with clause 9 highlighted. That was a clause that enabled them to fire him on the spot and run him out of the country on the next flight. Not only has he lost face, been shaken to the roots and acted like an idiot he now has a new nickname. He is now simply known as 'Clause 9'.

SATURDAY OCTOBER 6TH

Like many people I have total respect for fire-fighters and on the course I did earlier on in the year I know what dedication and courage these people have. We have a small fire station at the camp and the lads that man it are a friendly bunch. I am sure if called into action they will show those qualities in abundance. At the moment it is very quiet for them and so there are another two tasks that require their total dedication and courage.

The first is the band that they have set up and last night during dinner we were forced to endure it. I have never seen people eat so fast. The music was annoyingly atrocious and after hearing it I can honestly say that I will never slag off 'the birdy song' ever again.

The second is to do with food. The lads never miss a meal and I am sure that when they see the word 'menu' they must think that it is a mandatory requirement to eat everything listed beneath it. We must have the heaviest brigade in the world here. God forbid if there ever was a fire in the musical store room as its right next to the canteen, or is that wishful thinking?

SUNDAY OCTOBER 7TH

At KPC, the newly-constructed power plant consists of 3 x 40 MW gas-diesel fired turbines. The power generated will supply the project and 17% (20 Mw) of the electricity generated will go to the National Grid. Today our turbine vendor got the instruction from his company to remove the tracking devices off them. It's common place for suppliers of major equipment to install such devices as it allows them to monitor their locations during shipping, etc. The vendor rep only gets to know their location once he is on-site and then he has to be left alone whilst removing them. They come in all shapes and sizes so trying to find one is just about impossible unless of course you're Ethan Hunt or James Bond.

MONDAY OCTOBER 8TH

According to Somerset Maugham the best way to overcome temptation was to satisfy it. As far as May West was concerned temptation was something you had to avoid unless you can't resist it, and Oscar Wilde reckoned he could resist anything but temptation. Well there has been a lot of satisfying and very little resistance going on in the canteen and materials yard. The main communication of the morning listed all the items that had recently been stolen from the project. It ranged from lamps, grinding discs and cable down to lunch bags. I can understand the majority of it but lunch bags, some people are more desperate than I thought. According to security managers, Stevie Wonder and Ray Charles, they are going to take a good long hard look into putting it right.

TUESDAY OCTOBER 9TH

A guy goes into a chip shop and says to the owner, "Gis a bag of fucking chips." The shocked owner replies, "You don't ask for things like that. Come on, let's change places and I will show you how it's done." They change places and the shop owner asks, "Could I have a bag of chips please?" The guy looks at him and says, "Fuck off, you wouldn't serve me." I got the required laughs and then I began the quiz night with the question, "What is the only team in the English football league that doesn't have a vowel in the first five letters of its name? It took some them a while to work out that it is Crystal Palace.

To name the year I gave the following clues: Euro Disney opened in Paris and Betty Boothroyd became the first woman to be elected Speaker of the British House of Commons. The hit song of the year was *Black or White* by Michael Jackson. There was a flood in Chicago and a fire in Windsor Castle. All that happened in the year of 1992.

For the last question I asked the teams to name on the only thirty-minute show to appear on Britain's ITV commercial channel but it never had a commercial break in it. Nobody got the answer. It was a show called *This is Your Life*. It was one of those shows that swapped over from the BBC.

WEDNESDAY OCTOBER 10TH

I was given a safety award today. I got it for noticing a possible threat to safety, and by doing something about it I was commended and rewarded. When our car was entering site we overtook a bus with about forty frozen people on it. As we pulled alongside the front of it the driver had the look of someone in a wind tunnel. I then noticed that his entire front screen had been removed. I couldn't believe what I was seeing. We pulled the bus over and called the safety department. The lads sorted it out and later I was told that thugs had smashed the window so the driver had cleared out the glass and continued onto work so that people could get to site. It must have been one hell of a journey. The driver got a polite chat and a different bus. The passengers got hot drinks and an hour off. I got a pen knife.

THURSDAY OCTOBER 11TH

Sam, one of our mechanical engineers went into the town today to get some music discs. Whilst there he had a quick look around the market and two new stalls caught his eye. The first one was selling boxes of grinding discs and the second one was selling readymade lunch bags. Tim, our materials control manager, was glad of the info. Sam never bothered telling Mario the catering manager as whoever is taking the lunch bags is doing us all a favour.

I gave the canteen a try for a change and behold there was a new chef serving. He is from Hartlepool in England but at first glance you would think Shanghai in China. He's called Dave and he seems to have a short fuse. I don't know why but all I asked for at the counter was, "Fi and Chi." When he got slightly agitated all I said was, "Why you no risen?" I don't think my Benny Hill impression went down to well with him as he stormed off.

FRIDAY OCTOBER 12TH

Well at least I won't starve. I now know how to ask for an apple (yablaka), orange (apesin), grape (vinigrab), pear (groucha), potato (kartoshka), cabbage (kapoosta), onion (look), carrot (markov), cucumber (agoorets), pepper (perets), tomato (pomidor), chicken (couritsa), sausage (kalbasa), fish (reba), egg (yietso), milk (malako), butter (maslo), cheese (sir), water (vada), chocolate (shokolad) and last but not least, beer (peva).

SATURDAY OCTOBER 13TH

The train track to KPC is now complete and before we go for a working commission we have to see what it's like. For me it was an adventure but for Brian, from safety, it was just an inconvenience. Mind you, when you have a head like a bag of spanners after a night on the piss it would be. We assembled in Aksai and then got on-board. The train had a ripe old smell to it and the seats were that hard if you were on them any length of time you would end up with an arse like a baboon. Having said that, Brian managed to sleep through the entire journey. When we pulled into the station at KPC his tongue was up against the window and his shoulder was covered in dribble. It was time to wake him up. I ushered all the lads off the train and lined them up on the platform at the window. When everybody was ready I banged on the window. As soon as Brian opened an eye I gave the nod and we all started to walk backwards and wave. He had no idea where he was but something told him to move fast. A few seconds later the train door flew open and he rolled out of it like a paratrooper from an aeroplane. The Kazakhs thought it was hilarious. To them he is now simply known as 'Freefall.'

SUNDAY OCTOBER 14TH

Today, Jim our piping engineer showed me a note from his new back to back. Jim has been on the job for a few years now and his radio number has always been 236. The new broken arrow called Paolo has come from a job where his radio number was 718 and so he has changed the shared radio over to that. His note to Jim was very polite and he was sure that he wouldn't have a problem with the new number and would get used to it in time regardless of all the people who had the number 236 for him. Jim then showed me his emailed response.

Dear Broken Brain,

236 has been my number for four years and that's what I have just set it back to. If you have a problem remembering it, then please use the following steps.

1. *Take a single sheet of A4 paper and place it on the table.*
2. *Take a pen and write the number 3 in the middle of it.*
3. *Multiply that number by 2 and write the answer to the right of it.*
4. *Divide the number you have just written by 3 and write it to the left of the number 3.*
5. *Memorise it.*

6. *Failing that fold the piece of paper up and place it in your pocket. When asked what your number is you can then retrieve it and read it out to them.*

Regards,
Jim.

MONDAY OCTOBER 15TH

I got stopped by Shanghai Dave from the canteen today. "Someone has been looking for you," he said.

"Does he have a name?" I asked.

"I didn't get it."

"What company does he work for?"

"I never noticed."

"What colour were his overalls?"

"Red, I think, or was it orange?" I have no option now so I have to ask, don't I. "What does he look like?" Now you think about what we Westerners think when describing anyone from Asia, well Dave hit me with the perfect response. "I don't know, you all look the same to me."

TUESDAY OCTOBER 16TH

After a crazy day on the recertification of lifting equipment it was quiz time. Our sponsor was some expat without portfolio that was in the country trying to sell get rich schemes to everyone. Anyway, just before the quiz began he handed me a sheet of paper that was full of questions and answers about investments, etc. He then proceeded to tell me that he wanted them incorporated into the quiz and if not he would withdraw his sponsorship. I can honestly say it was the most pleasurable "Fuck off" I have ever given to anyone. His follow up attempt to make amends went down like a lead balloon and soon afterwards he left the bar. One of the vendors stepped in with the required funds and so we were off.

For the opening joke I mentioned a young couple that were about to get married. They had decided to save the sex for the wedding night but the night before, as the guy gave his soon to be wife a kiss, he dropped his trousers. "See that?" he said. "You are getting that tomorrow." The girl never slept a wink and so on the morning of the wedding she went to see her doctor. "What's the problem?" she asks. "Last night my husband to be kissed me goodnight and then he showed me his thing and it's the first time I have seen one."

"Thing…" repeats the doctor. "You mean his penis."

"Err yes, his penis," says the girl.

"So have you got a problem with it?" asks the doctor."

"No…" begins the girl. "…it's just that about eighteen inches away from the tip of it are two big round things and I don't know what they are."

"Well," replied the doctor. "For your sake you had better hope that they are the cheeks of his arse."

For the opening question I asked the teams to name the A to Z of top goal scorers in the English premier league. The twenty-six answers are as follows; Anelka, Beattie, Cole, Dublin, Euell, Fowler, Giggs, Henry, Ince, Johnson, Keane, Lampard, McAllister, Nolan, Owen, Phillips, Quinn, Rooney, Shearer, Torres, Unsworth, Van Nistelrooy, Wright, Xavier, Yorke and Zola.

To name the year I gave the following clues: Simon and Garfunkel sang about Mrs Robinson and Cricketer Garfield Sobers became the first player to hit six sixes in one over. Jacqueline Kennedy got married to Aristotle Onassis. The Israeli commandos carried out a raid on Beirut International Airport and Richard Nixon became the 37th president of the United States. All that happened in the year of 1968.

The last question went like this; the year was 1998. When it started its journey it was worth three dollars. Six seconds later at the end of its journey it was worth three million dollars, what was it? It had them all going and one team did manage to get it. Baseball player Mark McGwire of the St. Louis Cardinals hit a record breaking seventy home runs in 1998. The actual baseball was sold at auction for three million dollars.

WEDNESDAY OCTOBER 17TH

I popped in at the local Trnava store today to get some music and I was almost sent flying by a few school kids on the run. By the looks of it they had just been spotted pilfering something and the chase was on. These kids don't seem to have the class for this sort of thing. I once remember when I was outside a well-known retailer in Stockton High Street and witnessed how it should be done. Three school kids were in a huddle and then one disappeared into the shop. Ten minutes later he came out with a bag full of stuff. He poured it into a rucksack and then handed the bag and receipt to one of his mates. He went into the shop and two minutes

THE ROBES OF FAILURE

later he was back out doing the same swap. I was going to move on but decided to stay and see what happened. Minutes later, kid number three emerges from the shop with a full bag. I waited for the three of them to get clear of the shop before confronting them. The panic disappeared from their faces when I told them that I was nothing to do with the shop I was just interested in their scam. They explained that they had twenty items on a list and the first went in and bought them. He would hand the bag and receipt to the second who would just enter the shop, refill the bag and then walk out without paying. The third would do exactly the same. If they got stopped then they had a fully paid receipt that matched the contents of the bag. In short they got sixty items for the price of twenty; simple and clever.

THURSDAY OCTOBER 18TH

Old Mick, one of our mechanical engineers, is strictly a field man. He spends very little time in the office and as far as he is concerned the PC is a tool of the devil. He hates being corrected by Word, he has no idea what Excel is all about and as for email, well he despises it. As far as he's concerned it's just a cowardly electronic way of passing the buck. If it was down to him all those time wasters that spend all day sending mails with 'fyi' as their only input, should be shot. Well today I showed him the devil's work. When he came in off-site for a cup of tea he was greeted by one of those transfers of responsibility emails. They are the nice little notes by so-called important people that have gone on leave or just can't be arsed to do anything that let everyone know who their designated dogsbody is. Mick read one from a British Gas manager and then forwarded it on to the lads in our office with a slight change of words. He wrote, 'For the next fifteen minutes I am going for a shite so while I am away big daft Andy Darragh will take over my roles and responsibilities.' I sent it on to our boss with a little note of what I needed him to do. Two minutes later he burst into our office and began screaming at Mick. He told him that there was no need whatsoever to tell the entire project about his bodily functions. He then stormed out but came back one minute later to say that he had just been told to call the manager in question. As he left Mick went into panic mode. He checked his email, asked us who got it and couldn't work out how our boss knew. As he began to shake I checked his PC. I then asked him if it was a new email or did he just modify the old one. When he told me that it was the latter I then asked him if he knew about Outlook's residual memory.

As he stared blankly at me I told him that if you modify a global email the system automatically sends the new one to everyone on the original list. With trembling lips he looked at his screen to see that the manager's email had gone to a worldwide distribution. "Well done Mick," I said. "You have just told thousands of people that you are going for a shite." Well that was it; he started to hyperventilate and rushed out of the office. He walked up and down the corridor for a while before rushing outside. Two minutes later one of the lads came in and said, "What's up with Mick? He's just lit up a fag outside and he's sucking on it like a laboratory beagle." A few moments later he returned to our office with the screams of our manager reverberating around the building. He slumped in his chair and was about concoct some lame excuse before our manager stormed in. Mick just about shit himself there and then and that's when our manager couldn't hold on anymore. He burst out laughing and we all followed. When I explained the joke I have never seen such relief on a man's face. He eventually told us that in his head he was already trying to work out a resignation letter and couldn't decide on whether to replace the word shite with crap or dump.

FRIDAY OCTOBER 19TH

As our visas are only valid for three months I had to apply for a renewal today so that meant I had to have another medical and HIV test. The medical took about one minute whereby I was asked a few simple questions and gave all the right answers. They then took the required blood and sent it off to the labs. I think I spent around five minutes in the clinic and for that the project will be charged the full rate. I suppose it's nice work if you can get it and out here somebody obviously is.

SATURDAY OCTOBER 20TH

I was on pipeline duty again today. According to the drawings nearly 400 miles of 24" pipe along with two pumping stations are going in so that the sweet stabilised liquids from KPC can be transported to an existing station at Bolshoi Changan. From there it's going for another 300 miles along an existing corridor to a tie in point at Atyrau. There is a lot of directional drilling involved and the crews we met were a great bunch. I was made welcome and I'm sure the newspapers and bars of chocolate I took must have had something to do with it.

SUNDAY OCTOBER 21ST

I have been learning the colours and in doing so noticed something unusual.

Colour.	Russian.	Kazakh.
Red	Krahsniy	Kizil
Blue	Galooboy	Kuk
White	Byehliy	Ak
Black	Chyorniy	Kara
Green	Zeelyohniy	Zhasil
Orange	Ohrahnzhiviy	Kizgilt Sari
Yellow	Zhyoltiy	Sari
Brown	Kahrichneeviy	Konir
Violet	Feeahlyehtahviy	Kulgin
Pink	Rohzahviy	Kizgilt

Now the colours on the Russian flag are red, blue and white so the Russian tongue they are Krahsniy, Galooboy and Byehliy. If you put the first letter of each of those colours together you get KGB. So there you are; the Russian flag spells KGB.

MONDAY OCTOBER 22ND

Now that the power plant has been commissioned and the tie-in to the National Grid has been working successfully for a few days the authorities have broken the required connection to Russia. That means the area will no longer have to be subjected to the usual power cuts initiated by their friendly neighbours. I am sure Putin will get to know soon as this isn't the Kazakhs' only surprise.

TUESDAY OCTOBER 23RD

A guy meets an old friend in a bar and is surprised that he only asks for a soft drink. "That's not like you at all. What happened to that guy who used to get hammered all the time?"

"I had to stop doing it as it was driving the wife crazy. I got to the stage where I used to go home in a mess with sick all over my clothes and—"

"Oh that's an easy one to get away with," interrupts the guy. "It used to happen to me. I would just put a twenty pound note in my jacket pocket and tell the wife it was from the person that was sick over me. You know, to cover the cost of getting my clothes cleaned. It works, believe me." The friend thinks it over and decides to give it a go. Several beers later he goes home and falls through his own door. When he gets to his feet the wife is standing right in front of him. She looks at the sick all over is jacket and shirt and notices the money sticking out of his pocket. "What's going on?" she asks.

"I met Bob in the pub and we had a few drinks. Anyway, this drunk bumped into me and was sick all over my chest. He apologised and gave me twenty pounds to get cleaned up." The wife looks on for a moment before saying, "I can see forty pounds in your pocket."

"Ah yes," says the guy "The other twenty is from the drunk that had a shit in my pants."

Yes, I was on quiz duty again and managed to put together a few good sports questions. What is the lowest number you cannot hit on a dart board with a single dart? If there are eleven teams in a football knockout competition how many will get a bye through the first round? In cricket, if every batsman was bowled out first ball then which batsman would be not out at the end of the innings?

The lowest number you cannot hit on a dart board with a single dart is twenty-three. You can get one to twenty easy, twenty-one comes from triple seven, twenty-two comes from double eleven but there is nothing that gives you twenty-three. Five teams get a bye in an eleven team knockout competition. That way six teams play to reduce it to three and in turn those three join the five that had a bye. If every batsman was bowled out first ball then batsman number eight would be not out at the end of the innings as he would never receive a ball. With number two at one end the first over would go to one, three, four, five, six and seven. With the over complete, number eight would go in to watch number two and the remaining order get out.

To name the year I gave the following clues: The space shuttle *Challenger* exploded shortly after lift-off and Prince Andrew got married to Sarah Ferguson. In Britain everyone watched the Live Aid concert. Argentina beat West Germany to the FIFA World Cup and Clinton Eastwood stormed into office as Mayor of Carmel, California. All that happened in the year of 1986.

I ended the quiz by asking; In 1899 Good Friday fell on Boxing Day, how come? A few teams managed to get the answer. On Boxing Day in 1899 a horse race called the Thorneycroft Chase was run at Wolverhampton. One of the horses in that race was called Good Friday and sure enough it fell.

WEDNESDAY OCTOBER 24TH

We were sitting outside the Trnava having a few beers when we heard the commotion. Some big daft mongrel was galloping towards the bar in pursuit of some mingy cat. Anyway, the cat entered the bar area and then leapt up the trunk of a nearby tree and just clung there. The mad mongrel attempted to reach it, failing that it barked at it for a while and then it eventually got tired. Rather than leave it just sat down, looked up and waited. The cat just calmly clung on to tree. This stalemate lasted for about twenty minutes and in that time numerous photographs were taken. In the end the dog got bored and left and the cat dropped to the floor and began to wash itself. We had a good laugh about it and it reminded me of the time I was clearing my garage at home when I felt the eyes upon me. A cat was sitting on the drive with that head-tilting puzzled look upon its face. As I went to chase it away I heard the barking and looked up to see a dopey-looking Alsatian dog tearing towards the both of us. The cat quickly looked to the dog, looked at my garage with a half-opened door and then waited. The Alsatian got within yards before the cat set off. He ran towards the garage and at the last minute leapt onto the door and then sprung up onto the garage roof. The daft-arsed dog ran into my garage. It barked for a few moments before searching the area. With a dumbfounded look upon its face it eventually skipped back down my drive. As I looked up I could have sworn that cat grinned before it disappeared.

THURSDAY OCTOBER 25TH

I got the new visa put in my passport today and the money men have started to realise the cost involved if we all have to go through this regime every three months. Common sense is going to have to prevail here as its obvious somebody somewhere is bending the rules to line their own pockets. Let the games begin.

FRIDAY OCTOBER 26TH

Our turbine vendor arrived on-site today but the tools he needs to do his job are somewhere in Uralsk. Apparently, when he drunkenly got off the plane and eventually explained his way through Customs the project buses had long gone. He then agreed a fee with a local taxi driver, put his bags in the boot of the car and went off to have a fag. When he returned he handed the exact project address over to the driver and settled down for a sleep. Two hours later he arrived on-site, paid the driver and went to get his gear from the boot. Shock, horror, it was nowhere to be seen. After a heated debate the vendor then realised he wasn't shouting at the driver that he had agreed the fee with at the airport. It then sunk in that he had climbed into the wrong car so frantic calls had to be made. They eventually managed to track the driver down and he said that he had looked for the vendor everywhere at the airport and couldn't locate him. The bag is now in the hands of project locals in Uralsk and someone will bring it to site tomorrow.

SATURDAY OCTOBER 27TH

Old Mick had fully recovered from his global email so I thought I would have a little fun with him. His head was full of nitrogen/helium leak testing. It's the system that the industry uses to test the mechanical integrity of hydrocarbon process pipework. As he was at his desk going through some test packs I went into the DOS system on my PC and entered his username. I then sent him a message to restart his PC. When he saw the little grey popup message on his screen he had no idea that it was me. He rebooted his PC and when he went to login I sent him a 'Hang on a minute, I'm not finished yet' message. He just looked at the screen and shook his head. I then asked him to check his CD drive, and he did. I then asked him to check all his cables, and he did. When he logged on and went back into his test pack I sent him a note asking, 'Are you sure you want to delete all the files in this folder?' Before he could select 'No' I sent him a note confirming that the files are now being deleted. When he cursed out loud, panicked and then attempted to turn the PC off I sent him a confirmation that all the files had been deleted. He protested his innocence to the office and just as his blood pressure was about to go through the roof I sent him a final popup. It simply read, 'Sit down, you daft twat and calm down.'

On a lighter note the vendor's bags arrived, minus the wine and cigarettes.

SUNDAY OCTOBER 28TH

The re-routing of the gas pipeline around the Russian border was completed today and now the shoe is on the other foot. Whereas before the Russians would just increase the tax on Kazakh gas as it crossed its border, at a whim they are now going to have to go cap-in-hand to keep receiving it. They desperately need that gas to keep their cities going so now they are going to pay, big style.

MONDAY OCTOBER 29TH

It's the last leg of the Golf Championships in China so a sweep has been organised so that some money can be added to the charity fund. I was asked to help out and so after getting Phil Mickelson for myself I went to see if the process group wanted a go. They have always complained about not getting a go of things and so I thought I would put it right. In the end I just wished that I hadn't bothered. I had over one hundred pieces of folded paper in a cup, a pen and a list of those golfers that were in the competition. The procedure is quite straight forward but maybe I just didn't get across right to James. "I have never done this before," he said, "So what do I need to do?"

"It's simple," I replied as I put everything on the table before him. "You give me five pounds. You pick up the pen and you then get one of the pieces of paper out of the cup. You open it up to see what player you have drawn and then you write your name against his on the list." After explaining all that I left him to it and went to chat to the other engineers. A few minutes later I returned to find that he still hadn't made a selection. He looked at me and then said, "It's not as easy as it looks is it?" I then stood and watched as he tried to pick a folded piece of paper out of cup by balancing it on the end of the pen. How thick can you get?

TUESDAY OCTOBER 30TH

An Irishman goes for a job in a kitchen and the chef puts him to the test. He places a cabbage, a potato and a knife on the table. "Which one is the odd one out?" he asks. "That's easy," replies the Irishman. "It's the cabbage."

"How the hell is it?" asks the chef. "You can make chips with the other two," he says.

We have quite a big Liverpool and Man Utd following out here so I opened the quiz tonight with a question for the Liverpool contingent. I looked into autobiographies written by some of their legends and picked the ones with a clue to the writer's identity in the title. So for starters they had to name the authors of Anfield Iron, Ray of Hope, Crazy Horse, Stand up Pinocchio and A Matter of Opinion. The answers to them all were Tommy Smith, Ray Kennedy, Emlyn Hughes, Phil Thompson and Alan Hansen.

To name the year I gave the following clues: Arthur Ashe became the first black man to win the Wimbledon singles' championship and Heiress Lesley Whittle was kidnapped. Saigon surrendered and Graham Hill was killed in an air crash. Ali beat Frazier in the 'Thrilla in Manilla'. All that happened in the year of 1975.

I ended the quiz with four anagrams that gave a clever clue to the person's actual name. The anagrams were 'Old west action, I am a weakfish speller, UN's said he's mad, Heil old fart.' The answers were Clint Eastwood, William Shakespeare, Saddam Hussein and Adolf Hitler.

WEDNESDAY OCTOBER 31ST

It's London and it's the year of 1605. Lord Monteagle receives an anonymous letter warning him to stay away from the opening of parliament on November 5th. Monteagle passes the letter to the Earl of Salisbury who the leaves it until the evening of November 4th before ordering a search of Westminster. Guy Fawkes is caught, tortured and executed. The King orders that the nation should celebrate his survival by burning fires. This tradition lives on today although the initial topping of the fires with an effigy of the Pope has been replaced by a guy. And that was how it went down in history. It was a conspiracy, I hear you say and I would have to agree with you. That said, I am in my room on the camp thinking back to a certain Halloween not too long ago.

We had spent the night in Thornaby, causing the usual havoc when Keith turns to the gang of eight assembled and asks if anyone wants a jacket potato. Eight nods are followed by a short walk to a house on the end of a nearby street. We were told that his auntie and uncle lived there and they were both very house proud. It was just a reminder for us to take our shoes off and leave them in the passage. Keith opens the door for us and we all pile in. Shoes off we make our way into the front room to find an elderly couple sitting before the television. One of the lads takes a step forward and the woman screams. In a panic we all shout for Keith. That was when we heard the lock on the door click followed by it being slammed shut. We now realise we are in the house of total strangers. As the guy in the seat reaches for an ornamental poker by the fire we turn and run. Our shoes have been scattered all over the passage and Keith is nowhere to be seen. What followed resembled something out of a Norman Wisdom film. As I played tug of war with a living room door that now had a poker sliding backwards and forwards through it, everyone else fought for the rights pair of shoes. The screams got louder and louder. Eventually we sorted it and the door was almost ripped off its hinges before we ran out onto the street and then out of the estate. It took a while for the fear to turn into side-splitting laughter.

THURSDAY NOVEMBER 1ST

The journey home was a bit of a disaster. We were taken to the airport in the early hours, checked in and then told that there was a fault with the plane. That meant we had to get back on the buses along with those that had arrived so we could come back to camp. Our bags remained at the airport and this just had trouble written all over it. Anyway, by the time it was sorted and after we had endured another bus journey back to the airport, we took off. We landed at Stansted airport around midnight. When the luggage arrived on the carousel it immediately became apparent that it had been tampered with. All kinds of things had been stolen from all the canvas type bags and cases. Luckily I had a solid shell Samsonite one but even that had all its locks crushed. Nobody bothered to fill out any forms as they knew it would be a waste of time. Some people did take photographs so that they could be shown to the management upon our return to site but once again it would be futile. Connecting flights had been missed, there were no trains or buses and all the hire cars had gone. We were offered hotels but I had no intention of stopping. I wanted to keep moving so I went over to the taxi desk and asked how much it would be for a cab to take me to Teesside. I was told three hundred pounds so I just said 'ok'. The guy at the desk did a double take and then rang the drivers to see if one of them would do it. By the time they found one, two of the lads who had heard me order it wanted in. So ten minutes later the three of us were on our way home for one hundred pounds each. I got there just after five am and it was money well spent.

TRIP TEN

THURSDAY NOVEMBER 15TH

I met an old face on the way to the airport. Simon, the welder that got married back in June, was on his way home. We talked about married life, and without thinking I mentioned the condom that was pushed into his arse with a pencil. I thought the joke would have been out by now but by the look on his face it hadn't. I have never seen a man so relieved. He never mentioned it and so for the last few months he thought that someone had shagged him. He was still in shock when we said our goodbyes.

FRIDAY NOVEMBER 16TH

To assist the project and the locals, twelve kilometres of new road have been put down. Today, we bypassed a localised working commission and went straight for a state commission. It means that the roads in question are now recognised on the national register and receive the appropriate identification. It was one of the easiest handovers I have been involved in and it was all down to Patrick, a top-drawer civil engineer and a bottom-drawer clown. During the commission we talked about keeping fit and he told all those present that he never used gyms but had a dedicated regime that he could do in his room. He looks fit and so whatever it was it seemed to be working. That was blown out of the water a few hours later. I was on my way back from the gym and when I got to the accommodation block I was met by chaos. The corridor was full of people shouting and screaming as a security guy was working his way into Patrick's room. His frantic calls for help had set things in motion and a few minutes after I got there I saw the reason why. Patrick was standing in a t-shirt and shorts with pads strapped to his arms and stomach and he was shaking like someone getting an electric shock. He was using those electric pulse training things that work your muscles while you just sit on your arse. Anyway Patrick had set them too high and his arms were shaking so much he couldn't turn them off. As he wobbled around the room using every expletive known to man the lads that had assembled did what all caring colleagues would do. They all got their mobile phones out and recorded it so that they could send it into a TV show to get some money. Eventually, he was switched off and left in a heap on the floor.

SATURDAY NOVEMBER 17TH

Some of the lads have started to look at their rotas to ensure they don't cop for any tax. I just showed them an article in the newspaper. Some guy in Evesham has had his tax return rejected by HMRC because he had failed to answer one of the questions incorrectly. In the section where he had to list his dependants he wrote, *'Two million illegal immigrants, one million crack heads, four million unemployable Jeremy Kyle scroungers, one million criminals, six hundred and fifty idiots in Parliament and the whole of the European Commission.'* The HMRC sent him a note to say that his answer was unacceptable so he has just replied to it with the question *'Who did I miss out?'* We need more like him.

The video of Patrick's training regime is on the network and it's getting loads of hits.

SUNDAY NOVEMBER 18TH

My thirst for knowledge got dented a little today when I learnt that the Russian word 'Bolshoi' simply means 'big'. So the world famous Bolshoi Ballet is simply a Big Ballet. I'm not knocking its incredible dancers it's just that when you strip things down they really do have simple meanings and the mystery, drama and romance of it all just disappears. If you need convincing then Giuseppe Verdi translates as Joseph Green, Antonio Banderas becomes Tony Flags and Rafael

Nadal is Ralph Christmas. It just doesn't have the same ring to it anymore, does it?

MONDAY NOVEMBER 19TH

This morning we all opened up Outlook to see a 'Be Careful' email from the safety department. Two people had been attacked over the weekend. The first was badly beaten on his way from the market and the second got into a taxi that took him to a remote area where two people were waiting to give him a good hiding. Both attacks were carried out during the hours of darkness and alcohol was mentioned. Although the injuries are not serious it hasn't done a lot for project morale. The police have been informed and according to those in the know the town, is attracting migrants looking for work and when none becomes available they start to look for easy targets to fund their stay. According to our drivers the police have asked all the taxi drivers in the town to inform them whenever they see such gangs on their travels. It's co-operation that has worked before in that the taxi driver calls it in and the police go and pick the gang up, take their details and then drive them a few miles out of town. The police politely inform them of what will happen if they ever come back and wish them well for the journey they are about to take. We have been assured that the clean-up will take a few days and the locals on our project are going to great lengths to assure everyone that it's nothing to do with the town's folk. Maybe it isn't but right now that's little comfort for the two lads that got the kicking.

TUESDAY NOVEMBER 20TH

Two monkeys get into a bath. The first goes :Oooh oooh ahh ahh oooh oooh ahh ahh," so the second replies, "Well put some bloody cold water in."

As I asked a question in the last quiz about Liverpool autobiographies the lads have been swatting up on Man Utd autobiographies, so I opened with a question about famous football quotes instead. I asked them to name the people that said the following, "When the seagulls follow the trawler, it is because they think sardines will be dropped into the sea." "You don't win anything with kids." "I couldn't settle in Italy – it was like living in a foreign country." "I spent most of my money on birds, booze and fast cars. The rest I just squandered." "Some people believe football is a matter of life and death. I'm very disappointed with that attitude. I can assure you it is much, much more important than that."

The answers were Eric Cantona, Alan Hansen, Ian Rush, George Best and Bill Shankly.

To name the year I gave the following clues: The FIFA World Cup took place in West Germany and Patricia Hearst was kidnapped by the Symbionese Liberation Army. Charles de Gaulle Airport opened in Paris, Lord Lucan disappeared and there was a royal kidnap attempt. All that happened in the year of 1974.

I ended the quiz by asking: In 1971 the longest ever six iron shot in golfing history took place. Who took the shot? Where was he when he took it and for a bonus give or take ten yards, how long did it travel? The shot was taken by astronaut Alan Shepard from the surface of the moon and according to him the golf ball went 'miles and miles'.

WEDNESDAY NOVEMBER 21ST

The wife went to see one of those mediums, or psychics, today. She likes to be told a few 'You are going on a long journey' or 'I see the letter J' stories before handing over some money. I'm not sceptical I'm just slightly poorer, fifty quid a shot is a good rate for storytelling. I can't understand what people see in all this type of crossing to the other side or psychological healing magumba. If you ask me I am on the side of Ray Parlour and Groucho Marx. When England manager Glenn Hoddle employed Eileen Drewery to heal his squad she never got past Ray Parlour. With her hands hovering over his head she asked, "And how can I help you?" Ray simply replied, "Short back and sides and straight across the ears please." When a medium told Groucho Marx that she was the answer to all his questions he simply asked, "What's the capitol of North Dakota?"

THURSDAY NOVEMBER 22ND

Maybe it's because the shops in town have been a little quieter, or the bars have been empty or the taxis not so busy, but the police have advised the project that they have removed all the undesirables from the town. Maybe because it's Friday tomorrow and the weekend is almost upon us, today would be a good day to announce the all clear. Maybe I'm just being a little cynical.

FRIDAY NOVEMBER 23RD

The clever catering people have come up with improved lunch bags for those people that don't want to endure the bus journey back to the camp and the chaotic queuing system. They approach everything like they do in a car. If there is one lane then they put three in it, etc. Anyway I picked cheese and Jim, our piping engineer, opted for ham. Mine ended up in the bin and Jim's ended up being the focus of an email he sent to the catering manager. He wanted to know what tool they had used to slice the meat so thin. He also asked for the calorific value of the six kernels of corn that were dumped upon it. He went onto mention that the stale bread had been put to use as a door wedge but he couldn't do anything with the orange. The reason given was that it looked like some slip of a waitress had cunningly sucked its internals out before carefully blowing it back into shape. The supplied fizzy drink, flavour unknown, was put to use as a desk stain remover and the mini yoghurt was giving the toilet a run for its money in trapping flies. He hasn't received a reply as of yet.

SATURDAY NOVEMBER 24TH

We never got off the camp today. We got in the cars as usual this morning but there was a red flag on the barrier of the camp. The snow ploughs had been sent out and they just about made it to site. The message that came back was a simple 'don't bother'. So we turned away from the walls of snow and went back to bed. A few of the 'I just want to get the job done' gang stopped long enough for their voices to be heard on the radio but it soon went quiet. I don't know why the project hasn't handed medals out to them all yet as it would save on a lot of time, and money, and earache, and bullshit.

SUNDAY NOVEMBER 25TH

I was handed a book of Russian poetry today and one of them stood out immediately. It was a war poem written in 1941 by Konstantin Simonov to his future wife, the actress Valentina Serova. Pravda published it in 1942 and many soldiers carried it with them.

Wait for me, and I'll come back!
Wait with all you've got!
Wait, when dreary yellow rains,
Tell you, you should not.
Wait when snow is falling fast
Wait when summer's hot

Wait when yesterdays are past,
Others are forgot.
Wait, when from that far-off place
Letters don't arrive.
Wait, when those with whom you wait
Doubt if I'm alive.
Wait for me, and I'll come back!
Wait in patience yet
when they tell you off by heart
that you should forget.
Even when my dearest ones
Say that I am lost,
Even when my friends give up,
Sit and count the cost,
Drink a glass of bitter wine
To the fallen friend –
Wait! And do not drink with them!
Wait until the end!
Wait for me and I'll come back,
dodging every fate!
"What a bit of luck!" they'll say
those that would not wait.
They will never understand
how amidst the strife,
by your waiting for me, dear,
you had saved my life.
Only you and I will know
how you got me through.
Simply – you knew how to wait –
No one else but you.

Konstantin and Valentina eventually got married but while he was reporting on the war she never truly waited for him.

MONDAY NOVEMBER 26TH

So that the project can manage the on-going safe work practices on a site they use a 'Permit to Work' system which is controlled in a permit office by a permit co-coordinator. A permit is a document that includes the scope of work that is being done and carries with it all the required back-up documentation to prove that risks have been checked, isolations are in place and safety tests have been carried out, etc. Depending on what type of co-ordinator you have,

permits can either be a document that will keep you safe or a document you don't have a cat in hell's chance of getting. Mark, our mechanical engineer, only wanted to change out two nuts on a non-hazardous open drains pump but he was up against a newly promoted local controller. Mark had spent an hour with him showing him his permit, risk assessment, isolation certificate, as-built drawing, birth certificate, passport details, references from two past work colleagues, his holiday snaps and the contents of his wallet and he still didn't get the permit. Apparently it had something to do with another non-related permit that was on the other side of the site. So that was it, he had just completed the commissioning waltz (one step forward, two steps back). When he returned to the office he removed his overalls and threw them on an available peg. He stood looking at them for a moment before declaring, "The robes of failure. That's all they are, the robes of failure." It got my attention as it was the same phrase used by Walter when I was offshore with him in Morecambe Bay. I mentioned it to Mark and he reckons that if anyone should ever write a book about this game then it would be a fitting title.

TUESDAY NOVEMBER 27TH

A woman answers the door to find her son's school teacher standing there. "How can I help?" she asks.

"I have come about little John and the bad language he is using in school."

"That will be those bastards next door," she answers before letting him in. The teacher goes into the kitchen and finds the father standing there.

"It's about little John and his language," says the teacher.

"It's those twats next door," he begins. "They really are a bunch of arse-holes. Hang on a minute and I will go and get him so we can sort it."

"Don't bother for now," replies the teacher. "I will have to fuck off soon as I have a class in fifteen minutes."

For the opening question in the quiz I asked the teams a good one about the BBC's TV quiz show called 'A Question of Sport.' In total, the show has had fourteen regular team captains, so I asked them to name them. The fourteen sportsmen in question are as follows: Cliff Morgan, Henry Cooper, Fred

Trueman, Brendan Foster, Gareth Edwards, Emlyn Hughes, Bill Beaumont, Willie Carson, Ian Botham, Ali McCoist, John Parrot, Frankie Dettori, Matt Dawson and Phil Tufnell.

To name the year I gave the following clues: France beat Brazil in the FIFA World Cup Final and the search engine Google was launched. Francis Albert Sinatra faced the final curtain, Bill Clinton didn't really have sex with that woman and Michelangelo's Christ and the Woman of Samaria sold for $7.4 million at auction. All that happened in the year of 1998.

For the final brain teaser I asked then about the buttons on touch tone telephones. Apart from the numbers there is a '*' and a '#' but what where those buttons originally planned for? The first was going to be a direct link to the police department, the second was going to be to the fire department but that idea was scrapped in favour of using three numbers.

WEDNESDAY NOVEMBER 28TH

The camp that has been built right besides our main production facility is nearing completion so today I had to go and see their certification team to make sure they had compiled all the required documentation for when we have to get acceptance from the local authorities. I was told by the lads that I just had to ask for someone called 'Midnight'. So upon entering their office and I was met by a smiling Indian. "You must be Midnight," I asked.

"No sir," came the reply. "I am ten o'clock." He then took me to meet the man in question. I then realised what the joke was. Midnight had the darkest skin I had ever seen and as for ten o'clock well he was a little bit lighter. When I mentioned it to them they went on as if it was a badge of honour. Nobody ever really acknowledged them before but as soon as they got the nicknames everybody chatted to them. It even helped them in getting things approved so they weren't complaining. When all said and done I found them both to be polite and efficient, and better still, they kept their heads still whilst answering questions.

THURSDAY NOVEMBER 29TH

Some of the locals in the office that work through local agents had their contracts renewed today. I thought they were annual contracts but actually they are only eleven months in length. The agents do this to avoid all the sickness and holiday payments that go with annual contracts. One local agent told me that on one job his company made the mistake of giving three girls annual contacts and nine months later they had all become mothers. The agent had to then pay for their maternity leave and their temporary replacements and such things are not covered in their contracts with companies. It seems harsh but I'm afraid it's a case of take it or leave it and not many are going to do that. They don't have such things here as unemployment benefit or job seeker's allowance. If you don't work you starve. Yuri put it in simple terms when he told me that to outsiders oil companies meant big houses and flash cars but to those on the inside it was bread and water.

FRIDAY NOVEMBER 30TH

In this month back in 1850 the Scottish novelist, poet, essayist and travel writer Robert Louis Stevenson was born. He is best remembered for the novels *Treasure Island, Kidnapped* and *The Strange Case of Dr Jekyll and Mr Hyde.* He is least remembered for his twelve pieces of advice on how to live a happy life.

1. Make up your mind to be happy. Learn to find pleasure in simple things.
2. Make the best of your circumstances. No one has everything, and everyone has something of sorrow intermingled with gladness of life. The trick is to make the laughter outweigh the tears.
3. Don't take yourself too seriously. Don't think that somehow you should be protected from misfortune that befalls other people.
4. You can't please everybody. Don't let criticism worry you.
5. Don't let your neighbour set your standards. Be yourself.
6. Do the things you enjoy doing but stay out of debt.
7. Never borrow trouble. Imaginary things are harder to bear than real ones.
8. Since hate poisons the soul, do not cherish jealousy, enmity, grudges. Avoid people who make you unhappy.
9. Have many interests. If you can't travel, read about new places.
10. Don't hold post-mortems. Don't spend your time brooding over sorrows or mistakes. Don't be one who never gets over things.
11. Do what you can for those less fortunate than yourself.
12. Keep busy at something. A busy person never has time to be unhappy.

SATURDAY DECEMBER 1ST

Last month the technical interpreters had managed to negotiate a pay rise. All of them come to Aksai from other regions and so they wanted compensating for it or they were going to move on. Sure enough the project had listened with a sympathetic ear and an increase of one hundred dollars per month was agreed. Today one of those interpreters informed me that the landlord of the building they were all staying in has just put their rents up by one hundred dollars per month, loose lips and all that.

It's getting really cold here now and according to the locals the snow is on its way. They tend to use Moscow as a gauge for it. At the moment they have to endure blizzards so it looks like the thermal gear is going to get used.

SUNDAY DECEMBER 2ND

I have started on basic sentences in both languages now and its true what they say; I should have done something like this when I was younger. It's quite hard to maintain the enthusiasm after long hard shifts but somehow I'm still asking and learning.

(Eng) What is your name?
(Rus) Kak Tebya Zovut.
(Kaz) Senin atyn kim.

(Eng) My name is.
(Rus) Menya Zovut.
(Kaz) Menin atym.

(Eng) Nice to see you.
(Rus) Rada Vas Videt.
(Kaz) Seni korgenime kuanyshtymyn.

(Eng) What have you done today?
(Rus) Shto vy delali sevodnya?
(Kaz) Bugun siz ne istediniz?

(Eng) What do you want to drink?
(Rus) Sto Vy Hatite Pit?
(Kaz) Siz ne ishesiz?

(Eng) The weather is good.
(Rus) Haroshaya Pogoda.
(Kaz) Aua raiy ote zhaksy.

(Eng) The weather is bad.
(Rus) Pogoda Plokhaya.
(Kaz) Aua raiy ote zhaman.

(Eng) That's nice.
(Rus) Eto Horosho.
(Kaz) Barakeldy.

(Eng) Well done.
(Rus) Molodets.
(Kaz) Zharaysyn.

(Eng) Have a good journey.
(Rus) Horoshego puteshestviya.
(Kaz) Jolyn Bolsyn.

MONDAY DECEMBER 3RD

Winter has arrived. It hasn't just gently strolled here before quietly taking up position it's just crashed right into our laps. Temperatures plummeted during the night and the blizzards that came with it mean that the camp is knee deep in snow. The ploughs have been out to clear the roads and our cars now have arctic style tyres. All the potholes have been filled by ice and I have about four layers of clothing on. The journey to site was done in record time. Snow and ice have the opposite effect here. At home we come to a standstill but out here everything becomes much easier. I only saw one downfall on the way into work and that was a frozen dog by the roadside. Its bottom half was wrapped in ice and its top half struck a still pose that reminded me of that dog in the move trains planes and automobiles. It wasn't alone though as the birds had gathered to mourn its passing. All they needed now was the rising sun to thaw it out a little before they could tuck in.

TUESDAY DECEMBER 4TH

A little Indian walks into a bar with a big bright red and green parrot on his shoulder. The barman takes a step back in shock and then says, "Bloody hell, where did you get that from?"

"Asia," replies the parrot. "There are fucking millions of them."

I set the quiz off by asking the teams to name six British football teams that have a part of the human body in their name and they couldn't use Arsenal or Scunthorpe. They worked that bit out and luckily I got another laugh before they went to work on the answers Chest is found in a few teams so Manchester United was one. Mouth is in a few teams so Portsmouth works. Liver is in Liverpool, Heart is in Hearts and Head is in Peterhead. The hardest one to get is Chin because it's in Brechin and the pronunciation tends to trick people.

To name the year I gave the following clues: The Grand National was won by Corbiere and the best song was *Every Breath You Take* by the Police. Korean airliner KAL 007 was shot down after straying into soviet airspace and a nation-wide hunt for kidnapped Derby winner Shergar began in Ireland. At the movies we watched *Star Wars Episode VI, Return of the Jedi*. All that happened in the year of 1983.

For the final question I had put the following letter on their papers 'HIJKLMNO'. I then told them that the answer to that clue was five letters long, so what was it? When you look at the letters they got from 'H' to 'O' or put another way H_2O which is the chemical formulae for 'WATER'.

WEDNESDAY DECEMBER 5TH

There was a rumour going around today that we could be using clocking on and off cards. Most of us couldn't believe it as we thought we had seen the last of all that nonsense. There is nothing more degrading than watching people line up at a clock wait for it to reach an allocated time so that they could make a move. The last time I had to do it we just used the system. When we came on shift we would clock the cards of the nightshift that had already gone home as they had clocked our cards on. When we finished a shift we would clock their cards back on shift and when they eventually arrived they would clock our cards off. By swapping like this both shifts were paid extra. Yes, it's wrong but if companies want to treat humans like robots they deserve everything they get. Anyway, word was passed that if it was introduced we would refuse to use it on mass. It went quiet after that.

THURSDAY DECEMBER 6TH

Today I received my 'Conflict of interest' form. It's the sixth one I've had since joining the project. Basically it's a piece of paper with the usual company rules on it with a nice little section for me to enter the details of any presents anyone has given me. That is, any present worth more than ten dollars. Oil companies have introduced these since certain scandals came to light about the so called bribes or sweeteners people have received over the years. Some high fliers have apparently attended coke-filled orgies, been given golf clubs or seats at prominent sporting events, etc., etc. Thanks to all that pond life like me has to fill out this form every month. It would save a lot of time if they just had a tick box against the words 'fuck all'. Anyway, I completed mine in the usual fashion and handed it back in. To be honest it's a joke. Those in the know still get sweeteners and now they are a little cleverer at it. When all said and done I don't care what they get as long as people get jobs.

FRIDAY DECEMBER 7TH

Jim got back late from a meeting in Uralsk and it wasn't the safest of journeys. This is what he wrote in an email to the management:

'This is just to a not to say how effective the latest exhortation posters are ref car accidents, with the slogan "It could be any one of us" - particularly the one in the foyer showing a smacked-up Lada Niva. Please could you arrange a print of the Lada Niva poster for my office with the slogan amended to state "It could be any one of us - but I'm pretty damn sure it's gonna be me!"

The reason for this request is that I drove back up from Uralsk to KCC in the dark on Monday night, in a Niva. I would have informed you about all this sooner, but I had to wait for the shakes to subside before I could hit the right buttons on the keyboard. The problem is visibility from the car, in darkness. The nearest we came to providing you with a very significant upgrade to your existing poster was c. 6" — from a horse and cart moving at c. 6 mph. There must have been something wrong with the 1 HP engine or its alternator because, surprise, surprise — it was showing no lights at all! We swerved to get around and just avoided a truck coming the other way — what with the darkness and my limited Russian I couldn't make out quite what the farmer was shouting but it certainly wasn't "Happy Crimbo". From the way the horse was defecating as we swung by you could tell that it was not too trashed about the incident either.

Right through the journey the driver maximised the use of main beam, with which visibility is just about safe. However, it is a very busy road indeed morning and night and to travel the whole journey on main beam only creates just another safety hazard for the vehicles coming the other way – who then use their main beam on you to get their own back – and then we're all in the shit.

The other near misses included;

A tractor and trailer, spotted at c.20 m. could not go around due to oncoming traffic, and got close enough to do a quick MPI check on the trailer tailgate hinges (they failed).

Two wagons broken down on the carriageway – again no lights. Pulled up about 4 feet away.

A wizened old biddy stood on the road hitching. She jumped out of the way just in time. We stopped to see if she was OK. She had no teeth but we were unable to discover whether this was the result of the fall she had just taken or whether it was the bad diet during the war. She spoke little English and was clearly in shock, just repeating, "Geordie Twats", over and over again.

Your comments and action would be much appreciated.
Cheers – Jim'

SATURDAY DECEMBER 8TH

I saw just how strange severe temperatures can be today. At lunchtime it was below freezing on the gauge at site yet I was outside in a t-shirt. The sun was up, there was no wind and so there was no moisture in the air. It was dry and still and some of the distant scenery would be at home on any Christmas card. I spent a few hours in the contractor's office and by the time I had to return to our own the wind had got up. The one hundred metres I had to cover seemed like a mile. My face felt like it was on fire and my hands almost turned blue. All uncovered hair suddenly went as stiff as a board. My head, eyebrows, nose and ears suddenly began to tingle. After a breath taking journey that was done at an angle of sixty degrees I managed to get back into the warmth of our office. The first thing the security guard did was to pull an icicle from the cheek of my face. It had started out as a tear from my eye. He then grabbed his cup of coffee and beckoned me back to the door. He quickly opened it and launched the coffee into the air, and closed it again. Through the glass I watched as the liquid just evaporated.

We also had a working commission today on the camp that has been built right next to the main process facility. It went off without any problems. I am sure the fact that the management had spread the word that more jobs will become available once it's sorted had something to do with it.

SUNDAY DECEMBER 9TH

Some of the team has had to move into the camp today. It has an office complex at one end with a canteen in the middle with a linked accommodation block. The Brits and Yanks moved in without a fuss but the broken arrows took one look at the little box rooms and left. According to their contracts they have to receive certain items of comfort. Each room has to have a phone and at the same time be bigger than a telephone kiosk. Each room has to have hot and cold running water and at the moment the camp is producing a slightly warm liquid with a tint of brown in it. There has to be enough wardrobe space to accommodate a complete set of cheap suits but the ones in the camp are just about wide enough to hang a shirt in. Basically, the facilities don't meet their needs and as one of the head gaffers is also a broken arrow, he fully supported their quick exit. As for those that remained, the Yanks hit the canteen and the Brits set up a bar. The management was pleased with it all and were there to see the first bottled beers go down. They even stood and had their pictures taken under a sign that read 'Barlinnie.' The managers thought it was a cute sounding name. Barlinnie is the name of a prison in Glasgow, Scotland. I am sure they will make the connection one day.

MONDAY DECEMBER 10TH

Graduates Sarah and David have fallen in love and have been trying to keep their relationship a secret. It was going oh so well until this morning. They both arrived at work on time and in different buses but their jackets gave it away. As part of our PPE we get storm jackets and the first thing you do with them is write your name on the breast panel using a permanent marker. Today Sarah arrived as David and David arrived as Sarah. It remained like that for most of the morning. When it hit home they almost died of embarrassment, awww bless.

TUESDAY DECEMBER 11TH

A little bald fat bloke walks into a bar with a frog sticking out of his forehead. "How did you get that?" asks the barman.

"It started out as a boil on my arse," replied the frog.

I began the quiz by asking the teams to name the five English football teams whose name begins and ends with the same letter. The answers are Aston Villa, Charlton Athletic, Liverpool, Northampton Town and York City.

To name the year I gave the following clues: Alcatraz in San Francisco Bay the federal penitentiary closed and British spy Kim Philby went on the run. The film Dr No had its premiere in the United States. Frank Sinatra Jnr was kidnapped and in Britain it was a great year for a train robbery. All that happened in the year of 1963.

For the last question I had printed the seven letter word 'THEREIN' on their papers. I then told them that without rearranging any of the letters the word can give you ten words. Taking 'Therein' as the first one, what are the other nine? The answers are 'THE' 'THERE' 'HE' 'IN' 'REIN' 'HER' 'HERE' 'ERE' and 'HEREIN'.

WEDNESDAY DECEMBER 12TH

There had been a theft at the Early Oil Production (EOP) facility today and it took us a while to work out just what had been taken. When we met the security team we opened up the control room and found everything to be in order. As we scratched our heads they then pointed to the perimeter of the building. Someone had stolen the entire section fence, complete with guide poles. Not only that but they had then kindly dug the snow back into place and neatly smoothed it all over again. The amateur sleuths in the team soon got to work and found the tracks left by the getaway vehicle. It had a horse power of one at the front and wide sleek run flat tyres at the back. Rather than call out the military and encircle the town with roadblocks it was decided that the security team could go to town and check out the new houses that were being built there.

THURSDAY DECEMBER 13TH

I was informed that thanks to Jim the lunch bags have improved and so today I gave one of them a go. It filled a gap and only the two mini yoghurts were left and two of the girls fought over them. I then told them a story; it reminded me of when my kids, Elizabeth and Matthew, used to eat them. When they were very young it was always a post-meal tradition. On one particular day Elizabeth had been having the usual sister/brother dig at the dinner table and Matthew was just calmly letting it go by. Anyway, he finished his meal and went to the fridge to get two yoghurts. He took the lids off them both, put spoons in them and then brought them back to the table. He finished his, cleared away and was about to leave the room when I stopped him at the door. I asked Elizabeth to say something about receiving the yoghurt.

"You didn't have to do it," she snarled.

"Yes I did," he replied as he opened the door. "I checked the dates on them both and yours had expired." When he left the room she almost exploded.

FRIDAY DECEMBER 14TH

Barry from the piping department had been treated quite badly in a local restaurant a few nights ago so he roped a squad of us in to get his own back. Before he could go ahead with his plan he needed a tin of vegetable soup and a dozen bread rolls. The soup came in on the flight and the rolls were borrowed from the canteen. The table was booked, the meal passed by and we were all on our best behaviour. As the night lengthened Barry eased into a loud drunk acting mode and sure enough we were becoming the centre of attention for all the other diners. We were warned a few times by the staff before Barry went for the big scene. As far as anyone could hear he was about to be sick and he needed room. We all stood up and crowded around whilst he went through a fake spew routine. Out of view from everyone he threw the vegetable soup all over the table. When he had finished and collapsed back into his chair we all got the rolls out. As soon as we dipped them into the soup and began to eat the whole restaurant was in uproar. Some turned green, some just screamed and others made for the exits. The owner was about to call the police but he was told in no uncertain terms that there were plenty more volunteers waiting to take our places. Barry never got an apology but he did leave with a smile on his face.

SATURDAY DECEMBER 15TH

It's the last big get together before we all start heading home so what better time to get conned. When I got to the bar there was already a large squad in full flow so I ordered the round. There must have been about thirty people there so the barmaids went into hyper drive for a while. It was like watching a Tommy Cooper glass, bottle, glass bottle, bottle glass sketch. Anyway, when I get the cash out, one of the girls in the company takes it off me and tells me that she will sort it out with the staff. I grab my bottle and join in with the crack. A few minutes later the barmaids hand me the bill. When I told them that I have already paid it I get a line of blank looks. I look around and sure enough the girl that took the money from me has gone. When I asked everyone they all remembered her but no-one knew who she was with. So in the end this girl had blagged a few free drinks and then did a runner with my money.

On the good news front the brothers that had stolen the perimeter fence from the EOP's facility had been found. They are going to put it back tomorrow.

SUNDAY DECEMBER 16TH

Each unit has its own adopted dogs. It starts by the arrival of one or two and before you know it you have a pack. Nobody minds having them around and each day they get fed from one source or another. I usually take a stroll at lunchtime and end it on the bench outside our office where I feed whatever dogs turns up. Today that didn't happen for the reason that they had all been shot the night before. Apparently when local farmers report that their livestock is getting attacked by wolves the sites have to get rid of the dogs. The wolves go for the dogs and that can lead to the passing of things like rabies. Each project has a team of shooters and last night ours was busy. I only found out when Craig, one of the site safety officers told me I was wasting my time with the bag of meat I was holding. The dogs also get culled when their numbers become a nuisance to the site so I suppose there is a lot to be said for staying away.

MONDAY DECEMBER 17TH

The shift was only five minutes old when some local inspector burst into my office ranting and raving about closing the site down. He has one of our interpreters with him, he wants to see my qualifications as well as everyone else's on the project and I if I don't show him the project licences and agreements he was going to close down in the next ten minutes. After he managed to calm down I told him to never again stop one of our team members, I then asked to see his qualifications and I called security. When they arrived I informed them that they had about nine minutes to escort this fucking lunatic off-site. The interpreter was word perfect with his translation. After he had stormed out of the office I thought that would be the last of it but it wasn't. As the day went on

I received three phone calls from the managers of other sites that he had forced his way onto. They all gave him the same courteous reply that I had given and eventually so he ended up back in my office. He apologised for his rant and then went on to explain why. On three occasions he had attempted to get a job on the project and because he had failed he was very angry with KPO. So when his company had sent him to check on a few pieces of paper he wanted to show them what they were missing. It worked, I told him to fuck off and never darken my door again. I did wish him Merry Christmas but I never bothered waiting for the response.

TUESDAY DECEMBER 18TH

A guy parks his car outside a pub and was about to walk in when a young kid shouts, "Mind your car for ten pounds, mister."

"No need," he replies. "There is a Rottweiler on the back seat."

"Oh, it can put out fires can it?" replies the kid.

Three Alzheimer sufferers in a house and the first decides to have a bath. They fill it with water and then stop and think, 'Was I getting in this bath or getting out?' He then shouts to the other two "Was I getting in this bath or getting out? The second goes to check and halfway up the stairs he stops and thinks 'Was I going up these stairs or going down?' He then shouts to the third "Was I going up these stairs or going down?"

"I don't know," he replies. "I will have to come and check. I don't know, you don't get five minutes' peace in this house." As he got to his feet he knocked on the table. He then shouted to the first two, "Was that a knock at the front door or a knock at the back?"

Jesus stood up at the last supper and announced "I am now going to turn the water into wine." Judas then stood up and said, "Why don't you just put your five pounds in the kitty like everybody else?"

Well I set the quiz away with a question about horse racing. I asked the teams to name the five British courses that do not have any of the following letters in their name 'R.A.C.E.' the answers are Goodwood, Huntingdon, Ludlow, Plumpton and Taunton.

To name the year I gave the following clues: The music publisher EMI ends its contract with the *Sex Pistols* and Rock and roll 'king' Elvis Presley dies. The leader of the black consciousness movement in South Africa, Steve Biko, has died in police custody. Manchester United manager Tommy Docherty was sacked by the club's directors and Red Rum gallops into racing history by winning the Grand National for a record third time. All that happened in the year of 1977.

I ended the quiz by asking the teams about numbers in the English language; what is the only number whose number of letters is equal to its value. What is the lowest number that has the letter 'a' in it? What is the only number that has its entire letters in alphabetical order? The answer to those questions is four, one thousand, and forty.

WEDNESDAY DECEMBER 19TH

Наконец, я научился писать несколько фраз на русском языке. Надеюсь, однажды я смогу также писать и на казахском. Поэт Уильям Батлер Йетс сказал: «Мысли как мудрец, но общайся на языке народа». Если я научился писать на английском языке, возможно смогу немного писать то, что я выучил на русском и казахском.

I have finally learnt how to write a few sentences in Russian. I hope that one day I will be able to do the same in Kazakh. The poet William Butler Yeats once wrote, "Think like a wise man but communicate in the language of the people." Once I have learnt to do that in English then maybe I could get by with the little Russian and Kazakh that I have learnt.

THURSDAY DECEMBER 20TH

After going through the usual nonsense at the airport, everyone's in good spirits and looking forward to going home. I never drink while travelling home and this time was no different. A quiet flight for me was followed by picking up a hire car at Stansted airport and driving north. I enjoyed the drive until I got into Teesside. Chris Rea was on my side but the copper that pulled me over for speeding wasn't. I was just ten minutes away from home when I got to join him in his car. Did I know what the speed limit was? Did I know that I was doing eighty-three miles an hour? Did I know that I was about to be arrested for speeding and driving without due care and attention. It was just pointless me putting my case to this twat. I got the usual 'you have the right to remain silent but anything you say could be used in evidence against you' routine. "Do you have anything to say?" he said, pen at the ready. "Please don't hit me again, officer," I replied. When comedian Bernard Manning used that line he got a laugh but I didn't. As I was asked to leave the car he then said, "I hope your next journey is a slower one."

"And I hope your next shite is a hedgehog," I replied. I don't know if he heard it or not but by then I just couldn't care. Right now the guy was at the top of my shit list. If only he had stuck in at school and bothered to get himself an education he could have been doing something more worthwhile. Christmas Bah Humbug.

As I write this I think back to that professor and the jar of life. I am on my second beer and I have written rocks, pebbles and sand. Besides that are the people and places I have been over the year and I have to admit there isn't much sand there. I doesn't seem like five minutes have passed since I was standing on the deck offshore seeing the New Year in. That person is a little older and a lot wiser now. I am in a fantastic industry with incredible people and long may it continue. That said I have just one last task to complete. The year isn't over just yet so I wonder if I can get another beer in that jar.

3775011R00088

Printed in Great Britain
by Amazon.co.uk, Ltd.,
Marston Gate.